D0033962

The Art of
Heartaculture

authorHOUSE

1663 Liberty Drive, Suite 200
Bloomington, Indiana 47403
(800) 839-8640
www.authorhouse.com

The Art of
Heartaculture

Enrich your life, relationships, work,
and the planet by choosing to do <u>only</u>
what you want to do every moment.

Ellen Solart

First published by AuthorHouse 12/15/04

ISBN: 1-4208-0298-4 (e)
ISBN: 1-4208-0297-6 (sc)
ISBN: 1-4208-0874-5 (dj)

Library of Congress Control Number: 2004099364

Printed in the United States of America
Bloomington, Indiana

This book is printed on acid-free paper.

For Ivan

Acknowledgements

It has taken a long time to birth this book. Although I can't name everyone personally, I want to acknowledge all the individuals who have helped inspire and encourage me over the years through the trust and interest they have shown in my work. Thank you to all my counseling, mentoring, and workshop clients whose enriched lives have reflected the usefulness of Heartaculture principles and techniques, and whose urgings, "Hurry up with that manual!" have kept me plodding forward. Thank you to my parents Tessa and Chester Roberts for their consistent fostering and support of my self-reliance, and to my son Ivan for being my live-in guinea pig.

For the physical birthing of my book baby, I thank my co-creators: editor Kathryn Agrell and designer Lewis Agrell for their skills and dedication; my Dream Team for their crucial financial backing; and to Marci Golden, Deb Moore, and Andi Kramer Voogt for their valued friendship and feedback.

It is a joyous beginning! Now it is up to you, readers, to see where the journey will take you. Thank you for your interest.

Contents

Chapter One

It Is Your Choice

The choices you make on a day-to-day basis direct the course of your life. These same choices determine whether or not you satisfy your heart. No matter who you are, how old you are, or what your life circumstances are, at any given moment you can choose to make your life more fulfilling by picking different options. In our ever-changing world where the alternatives are infinite, the art is to know how to choose the ones that lead to your optimum experience.

"It is never too late to be what you might have been."

George Eliot

Being mindful of your daily choices, even the minute ones, and *how* you make them is the key. By staying attentive to all your options and following your innate, internal indicators, you can be guided by your inborn map to make moment-to-moment decisions that will best achieve self-fulfillment and maximum efficiency in your life.

▼▼▼▼▼▼▼▼▼▼▼▼▼▼
2

Expressing the Full Self

From the first moment of birth, an innate urge drives each of us to manifest all that we are capable of being. Impelled forward by an inborn knowing that there is somewhere to go and a way to get there, we come into the world ready to express the true and full Self in the best way possible every moment. Like a seed we respond to nourishment from our environment in order to root ourselves in life and seek whatever we need to fulfill our intrinsic potential.

Our natural inclinations grow more obvious as we survive the dependencies of infancy and develop the traits of our personalities. The latent buds of our unique characteristics develop as we explore various avenues of expression available in our homes, schools and communities. As adolescents and young adults, we gravitate toward the activities we enjoy, whether it is playing in the band, taking care of children, building model cars, organizing neighborhood games, working in the garden, conducting chemistry experiments, playing basketball, or volunteering at the local hospital. We are drawn to what quickens our spirits. Opening to life, we actively seek what makes us feel good, what nurtures our hearts and satisfies our souls.

When adulthood calls, we flap our fledgling wings, eager to become free agents. Separating from parents and teachers, we set off to navigate a course that appeals to us. Following the dictates of our hearts, we land in the places or situations we hope will be satisfying to us: a well-paid job, a marriage, college, a trip to some remote destination, a home-based enterprise, hanging out on the beach. No matter where we start or how strong our determination or ideals are, it doesn't take long before the necessity to earn a living, or the expectation that we "make something" of ourselves, leads to taking on responsibilities of job, family, and community.

Over the years the ideals and hopes we held as youngsters become more difficult to maintain. As we give way to the demands and routines of daily life, tending to our hearts and to our own self-expression and growth easily becomes secondary or even forgotten. Situational or cultural pressures are more influential than our hearts in dictating our choices. Instead of making what we want to do the priority, what we feel we need to do, or should do, takes precedence. It is easy, but need not be inevitable, to slide into an unfulfilling existence that may be productive, but not deeply satisfying.

Since this process of straying from the heart path is usually gradual, it is not always obvious. Life is too busy, too full, for self-reflection. The question, "Is my life all that it could be?" rarely gets asked. Even with the realization that life is not what was hoped for, it is often difficult to know how to bring about positive change. Often the beliefs "I've made my bed and now I need to lie in it," or "It is too late to change" keep us in dissatisfying circumstances.

> *"Every child is an artist. The problem is how to remain an artist once he grows up."*
>
> *Pablo Picasso*

It is my hope that with this book you will be inspired to review your current situation and make choices that align more fully with your heart. Stop now, take a deep breath and answer these questions: Is my life all that I would like it to be? If I had all the necessary resources and anything is possible, how would I change my life?

Making Choices in Alignment with Your Heart

If you had a movie of all that you did today and played it back in slow motion, the number of actions recorded and the number of things you do not remember doing would astound you. Most likely you would remember the major activities, but not the numerous lesser actions, most of which you were not even conscious of doing at the time. Think back to this morning when you woke up. Perhaps you opened your eyes, rolled over to look at the clock, sat up, pushed back the blanket, put your feet on the floor, stepped into your slippers, grabbed your bathrobe, put it on, tied the tie, patted the dog, and walked to the bathroom. All of this before you even got to breakfast! How many of these things do you remember doing? To count every action in a day would take much longer than the actions themselves.

For each thing you do, you make one or more choices. First you must choose to do whatever it is. Then there may be steps within the action that you must make choices about. For the familiar action of brushing your teeth, for example, you decide which brush to use, what and how much toothpaste, and what technique you will use—what kind of brush strokes. For the innumerable actions and choices you make on a daily basis, how conscious are you of even half of them?

We make most of the choices about the actions we take in our daily routine subconsciously. We do not usually think about putting our feet on the floor when we decide to get out of bed. We rarely contemplate how much toothpaste to use or what kind of brush strokes we will use to clean our teeth. We do it by rote. After making choices about an action the first time, the pattern is set and repeated automatically.

Not all choices are equal in significance, but all choices are important. Each choice has its consequence and each choice leads to other choices and consequences. How you take care of your teeth will affect their health and appearance. If they aren't healthy, you will need to choose whether to go to a dentist or not. Which dentist you decide to go to will determine how much you will pay for services and how well the services are performed, which will affect your financial situation and physical well-being, which will affect . . . and so on.

Each time you are aware that you are making a choice, you have the opportunity to choose what you want or don't want. When your daily routine is mostly a matter of habit—doing what you are accustomed to doing without asking yourself if each action is something you really want to do right then—you are forfeiting your power to make your life more of how you want it to be. By checking in with yourself about what feels right each moment, you stay attuned to which choices serve you best in getting more of what you want.

> *"Cherish your own vision and your dreams as they are the children of your soul, the blueprints of your ultimate achievements."*
>
> *Napoleon Hill*

When your choices take you toward what you desire, toward where your hopes and dreams lead, your spirit is nourished and your life force thrives. On the other hand, each time you do something you do not want to do, your life force is diminished to some degree. If over a period of time your choices lead you away from what you really want, your passion for life will not be sustained. A subtle shifting bit by bit—saying yes to the things your heart cries no to or saying no to what your heart yearns for—can lead to a regrettable realization down the road that life is not what you hoped for. Even when you have everything materially that you need to live well, and everything is going along smoothly on the surface, you may have no passion or deep satisfaction. You may have an existence that is tolerable, even reasonably happy, but is not fulfilling.

Look into the faces of the people around you. Some people are radiantly alive. They usually have smiles on their faces and their eyes are bright and sparkling. Other people are barely present, their eyes shuttered or glazed. Perhaps they grumble or don't look at you directly. We all have times of sadness or heaviness, but when we are truly enjoying our lives, our usual cheerful and positive disposition will show it.

Failing to pay attention to the clues along the way that indicate when we are straying from our heart's path can lead to a rude awakening—an event or situation, which presents itself full blast to get our attention, that we can't ignore or brush aside. It may be the unexpected loss of a long-held job, the discovery of a spouse's infidelity, or a heart attack that does the rousing.

At those moments we are suddenly unhinged from our daily routine and forced to cope with the immediate situation. The shock of the unexpected momentarily frees us from the ordinary and thrusts us into a fresh perspective. From this new vantage point there is the opportunity to evaluate the overall picture and look differently at our options. It is at these points we can choose to put a Band-Aid on our situation and blithely continue along the same track we were on, or seize the moment and ask, "How can I get more of what I really want?"

There is no need to wait for one of these awakeners to procure more satisfaction from your life with less effort. In the deepest part of yourself, in your "heart of hearts," lies the secret for achieving your greatest happiness. Here lies your connection to your innate potential and to the rest of the universe. At any given moment a part of you knows the best and shortest route for reaching your true desires, the desires motivated by your innate drive to fulfill your full potential and purpose in the world. It is when you are on the path dictated by this primal urge that you are the happiest. **Expressing your true Self every moment is what real freedom is all about.** The natural inclination is to strive for this ideal even if you don't succeed. Making a choice once in a while that isn't in alignment with your true desires won't affect your satisfaction a great deal. It is the cumulative effect of your daily choices that lead you on a path in alignment with, or away from, your heart.

Living by Internal or External Motivation

At a time in my life when I had everything that I thought would make me happy—a family I loved, a comfortable house, wonderful friends, and success in my work—I felt dissatisfied and angry. When I first admitted to myself that this was the case, I rationalized that I was tired, it was PMS, or I was under stress and all would pass. When I continued to be irritable and short-tempered and could no longer stand to live with myself, I

> *"The definition of insanity is doing the same thing over and over again and expecting a different result."*
>
> *Albert Einstein*

sat down and assessed my situation. In looking at all the possible causes for my anger, I first considered whether or not it was someone in my life who made me angry. My husband, in-laws and sometimes my friends and clients irritated me occasionally, but my anger wasn't about them. Then I considered all the things I was doing, all the choices I was making. In addition to maintaining a household, I had appointments with clients and on-going activities with family and friends. I liked doing these things, or at least I didn't mind doing them.

The source of my dissatisfaction wasn't an obvious external factor. It was only when I looked inward and explored my deeper feelings that I discovered it wasn't the

▼▼▼▼▼▼▼▼▼▼▼▼▼▼

choices themselves, but how I made those choices that kept me from feeling satisfied. It was the how, not the what.

Even though I liked most of what I did, I wasn't doing the things I really wanted to do. Most often I responded to what I thought I should do to have the lifestyle I wanted. I did what I thought I should, when I thought I should, to keep my family and clients happy and to have a well-run household. I ironed my husband's shirts when he asked me to because I wanted him to be happy. His happiness contributed to my happiness. I didn't mind ironing. I cleaned the house, made meals, arranged for repairs or needed services, and paid the bills on time because I wanted an efficient household. I talked on the phone to clients about their problems, lunched with my in-laws, and played games with my son. All things I enjoyed doing, but not necessarily when I wanted to do them. I responded to the requests made of me. I did these things because I liked the idea of doing them. I liked the idea of pleasing the people I cared about. Were these things I really wanted to do at the time? I no longer knew.

The "shoulds" ran my life and they were the "shoulds" of my own making. I acted out of what I believed were my best choices to get what I wanted. My beliefs, however, were founded on my conditioning, what I learned about how the world worked from my parents, teachers, peers, and society. At the time I didn't know there could be a different reality. I only knew something had to change.

In desperation, I made a revolutionary vow: I would do only the things I wanted to do and only when I wanted to do them. Period. Little did I realize then what I was saying or getting into. Little did I know I had discovered a major clue about how to work with the universe to maximize results while minimizing effort. Through the years of living my vow, my life evolved from being somewhat happy to joyful, as did the lives of the clients and friends who were the willing guinea pigs of what developed into a specific way of making choices.

This way of making choices is what I call **Heartaculture**. It is the practice of basing decisions on what you desire, not on what you reason. You act from what "feels best" rather than what "thinks best." **Heartaculture is the art of making moment-to-moment, internally motivated choices. It is the art of continuously attuning to your heart while conducting your work and personal life.**

Internally motivated choices are rooted in innate or intuitive knowing. They originate from your true desires: the deeper awareness of what best serves you in achieving self-fulfillment. When you do only what you want and what feels best, you permit the expression of your true Self and generate the best possible harmony, in the long run, with the world around you.

"Even more than we are doers, we are deciders."

Ralph Blum

Perhaps you think that what you do is what you want to do most of the time. **What you think you want, however, and what you really want in your heart of hearts may be very different.** Your environment and conditioning affect what you believe is "right" for you. Your beliefs in turn influence what options you consider and what choices you make. If you grow up in a middle-class suburb, your expectations for your future and your ideas about what options you have and what you think you want may be very different from your expectations if raised in an economically deprived area of a city or small rural community. When all of your family members and friends go to college because it is the thing to do, you know you will go to college too. You don't ask yourself if it is really, really what you want to do. You go along with the preset program assuming it is your best choice. If the standard of success in your immediate culture is to be a foreman in the local factory, the option of attending college may not occur to you. You may never ask yourself whether you want to work at the factory or go to college. You assume you will get a job at the factory because you believe your future hinges on it. **Decisions based on logic, beliefs or expectations are externally motivated choices.**

An externally motivated choice may be aligned with your true desires, but not necessarily so. You think college is a sensible step toward getting the job you want, and it also happens to be what you really want to do in your heart of hearts. Likewise, internally motivated choices may also make rational sense. For example, you really like the campus of your state college and going to school there is also economical. The difference is how you make the choice. What is your primary motivator? Do you choose to do the rational thing, which incidentally also feels good? Or do you do what feels best, which is a reasonable thing to do as well?

"You have brains in your head, you have feet in your shoes. You can steer yourself any direction you choose."

Dr. Seuss

When you live your life using the ideal of Heartaculture, all your choices will be internal choices. You'll only do what you wish to do and what feels good to do, whether it makes rational sense or not. This ideal is meant as a goal to aim for, recognizing that to achieve it fully in our current culture and commonly held worldview may be difficult.

Our lives are mired in layers of "shoulds." It is hard to extricate fully from this reality. What matters most is that your life is more and more what you want it to be, that your satisfaction deepens and increases. The purpose of this book is to help facilitate this process. By consciously practicing Heartaculture, even at a minimal level, you will amplify your life force and enhance the quality of your life experience. As your commitment to act from your desires increases, so will your energy and passion for life increase. Over time your life will metamorphose to be more fully what you wish it to be.

Exercise 1

How to become more conscious of the choices you are making

1. Pick one activity from your normal day and list every action you take to complete it.

Example

Activity: *Washing the dishes*

Actions:

a) Fill dishpan with water

b) Put soap in

c) Put dishes into water

d) Wash each dish

e) Rinse each dish

f) Place washed dishes into drainer to dry

2. List all the choices you need to make to complete each action.

Example

Choices:

a) To pick up the dishpan

b) To put dishpan into the sink

c) To turn on the water

d) How hot the water will be and how much water to use

e) What soap to use

f) How much soap to use

g) When to put dishes into dishpan

h) Which dishes to do first

i) What sponge to use for washing, etc.

3. Count the choices you make for this one activity. How many of these choices do you make consciously? How many of these choices do you make without thinking about them?

4. The next time you do this activity, make each choice consciously. Say to yourself, "I choose to (name the action)," for each of the steps you take. For example: " I choose to pick up this dishpan. I choose to put it into the sink. I choose to turn on this much cold water. I choose to turn on this much hot water. I choose to use this soap," etc.

Although your life would become very tedious if you stopped to consider every little action individually all the time, it is important to be aware that each choice you make, whether you are conscious of making it or not, can affect the outcome of your action. When you want to improve an aspect of your life, to make it more effective or satisfying, be sure all of your choices are the ones you wish to make.

Exercise 2

What motivates your actions?

1. List all the things you did today (or yesterday) on a sheet of paper.

2. Review the list and consider each action individually. Was this action something you really wanted to do at the time? If so, put a "yes" next to it. If not, put a "no."

3. Now review the list again and after each "no" write the reason you chose the activity in spite of not wanting to do it.

If you did most everything because you wanted to, your day was mostly internally motivated. If most of what you did wasn't what you wanted to do at the time, you were primarily externally motivated.

Chapter Two

Discovering Your Heart

Most everyone has experienced times when they consciously "followed their heart" and celebrated the results afterwards. These are the moments you especially remember, because you had to make a special effort to do what felt best, not what seemed to be expected of you or what reason told you was right.

For example, imagine reaching a fork in a road where the sign indicates that your destination is to the right. Turning right does not feel good to you. Instead you want to turn left. This does not make rational sense but feels better to you than taking the logical choice, the road to the right. Fighting your mind and following your feelings, you turn left. Later you discover that the bridge

"Think of yourself as an incandescent power, illuminated and perhaps forever talked to by God and his messengers."

Brenda Ueland

on the right-hand road is out. If you had taken it, you would have needed to turn around and go back to the fork and take the unmarked detour to the left. There was no way for your mind to know this, but your heart somehow did and let you know through your feelings.

Through experiences like these, you would think we would learn to trust ourselves, to give credence to the knowing that comes through our innermost feelings, not just occasionally, but daily. If it works once or twice, why can't it work all the time?

There is no need to wait for our external authorities to validate what our own experience is already telling us, even if solid scientific evidence is just around the corner. We humans are part of a universal unity in which everything is connected. Each of us is linked to the whole and thus joined into the universal consciousness. Like being plugged into an infinite database, we each have access to what is going on everywhere all the time, both in the material and spiritual realms. We can access this information easily and know what is best for us at any given moment.

Acknowledging Your Desires

Your heart is that part of your being that computes whatever is going on in both your immediate and greater worlds and registers its knowing via your feelings. The "heart" I'm talking about here is the feeling center that the ancient Egyptians revered over the brain as the site of intelligence, the "spiritual mind." By trusting your heart all the time, the occasional synchronistic or exceptionally opportune occurrences usually dismissed as "coincidence" can be your normal on-going experience.

Whether you heed the messages from your heart or not, they are there. Long before your logical mind has any clue or can come up with reasons for your knowing, your feelings will tell you what is happening or what will happen. By paying attention to sensations in your body or an "irrational shift" in your emotions, you can know when or when not to trust a stranger, when something has happened to a loved one, when you are being betrayed, or when you are not physically safe. You feel these things in various ways both physically and emotionally—sometimes in your gut, upper chest or in your entire body. You may feel them as joyfulness, lightness, heaviness, sadness, anger, restlessness, or anxiety.

All your feelings are important indicators of what is happening to you and around you, but it is desire, specifically, that Heartaculture is based on. **As a synthesis of your deepest soul urges and whatever is affecting you spiritually, psychically, emotionally, mentally and physically, your desires access most effectively your heart's knowing about which actions or options serve your best interests at any given moment.**

Desire is the force that impels you toward satisfying your needs and fulfilling your destiny. Whether you are conscious of your desires or not, they motivate all your actions. Think about what motivates you to get up in the morning, take care of your children, go to work, write a poem, talk to a friend, go swimming, eat

> *"A man is a success if he gets up in the morning and gets to bed at night, and in between he does what he wants to do."*
>
> Bob Dylan

ice cream, trade on the stock market, or paint the house.

One or more levels of desire motivate every action. You may get up in the morning most obviously because you want to empty your bladder. But you may also want to get on with your day or meet a friend for breakfast.

These desires may be prompted by more subconscious desires—to be healthy, to feel useful, or to be loved—which may be fueled by the even more basic desires to survive and to be fulfilled.

By acknowledging your desires, you can find your heart. Although not all desires are equal, it is by giving credence to each one equally that you clear the path to the different levels of the heart. As you open to a desire, no matter how trivial or warped it may seem, it leads you to the next level of desire, which leads to the next, all the way through to your innermost spiritual urges—your true desires. It is your true desires that are your innate prime motivators. They are what impel you toward self-realization, to fully express your inner or true Self. These are the desires that give the flow to your life force. They are your spiritual will. By following your desires to learn what your heart wants, your "heart-will," you can more consciously and effectively choose what will fulfill you.

> *"Everyone who got where he is has had to begin where he was."*
>
> *Robert Louis Stevenson*

The motto of Heartaculture is: **Do only what you want to do when you want to do it.** Choosing to do only what you want to do, at the time that feels best to you, will put you in touch very quickly with the various levels of desire. Wanting to stay in bed a little longer in the morning, for example, may pose a conflict if you anticipate being late for work or if you do not go at all. One part of you may want to stay in bed, while another part of you doesn't want to face the probable consequences of doing so: perhaps a mark against you with your boss, missing an important meeting, or not getting paid.

When you give yourself permission to stay in bed as long as you want to, no matter what, you will discover which level of desire is pulling the hardest. Perhaps you will find you don't want to stay in bed long. You really do want to get up and go to work. In that case, wanting to work is a stronger desire at that moment than wanting the sun to rise before getting up or snuggling longer with your partner. By giving in to your desires, your heart's priorities become clearer.

If you habitually force yourself out of bed each morning, not giving yourself a choice because your job requires you to be at work at a specific time, how does that make you feel toward your job? You don't give yourself the opportunity to know what you want. When you first took the job you knew you wanted it, but do you now? You may begin to resent work because you feel you have to be there. Giving yourself permission not to go if you don't want to each day keeps your choice in the present. Allowing yourself to stay in bed as long as you want to, then realizing you really want to go to work changes everything. When you want to do something, your attitude, the effort you put into your actions, the way you feel about yourself and others are all very different from when you don't want to do something but do it anyway. Giving yourself a choice makes you the power in your life, not the outside authority, real or imagined, that says you have to or else!

> *"We first make our habits, and then our habits make us."*
>
> *John Dryden*

If you find you want to stay in bed and not go to work, perhaps you want a change just for a day. If, however, the desire to stay in bed continues day after day, it may indicate something significant about what is going on (or not going on) in your life. Perhaps you are physically or emotionally depleted and need rest or nurturing. Perhaps some aspect of your life is unpleasant and by staying in bed you can avoid dealing with it, at least momentarily. Perhaps your job is no longer what you want.

This is the time to pay attention. Perhaps you already know you want a change in your life but haven't done anything about it. On the other hand, maybe you haven't realized how exhausted you are or how much you dislike your job. The desire to stay in bed is an indicator of what your heart knows. It knows you need a change. It also knows what choice or choices will benefit you the most in the long run.

Once you realize what your heart wants, will you follow its lead? If you realize you are exhausted and want rest, will you take time out, or will you ignore this knowing and keep pushing yourself? If you decide to give yourself some rest, what options do you see for getting it? Choose the option that feels the best to you.

If your moment-to-moment desires keep pointing to the fact that you want to change your work, list the options you see for yourself to do this. Taking even a small step toward a change will make a big difference. As you discover your desires and give them validity, you free more of your life force to give you more of the life you want.

Realizing Your Truth

When you question yourself about whether or not you want to do each action in your day, you become fully conscious of your current reality. This can be a happy revelation or a painful realization depending on where you are with yourself. If you are already accustomed to giving validity to

"You are never given a wish without also being given the power to make it come true."

Richard Bach

your feelings, this further fine-tuning will put you more in the immediate present, giving you greater power to make more effective choices. If you are in the habit of bypassing your feelings, going "along with the program" because it is easier at the moment, beginning to realize your truth can be very uncomfortable. Perhaps you need to ask yourself, "Do I want to know the truth? Do I want to take responsibility for my life?" My guess is that if you were attracted to this book, you are ready to know your true heart and take steps toward finding it.

Finding your true heart means to peel off all the layers of "stuff" that keep you from expressing the real you, your inner Self. These layers are the accumulated learned beliefs that you have about the world and yourself, which supersede your inner truth. They are all your conditioning from external sources about how you should be and what you should want for yourself.

Since most of us still have layers of conditioning burying our true hearts, we don't always recognize what we really want. We only know what we think we want. Our hearts, buried as they might be, can speak to us via our desires. Even when we don't consciously know what we want, we can be led, often wondrously and sometimes miraculously, little by little out of the maze of our conditioning, onto a direct path for fulfilling our innate potential.

"To decide, to be at the level of choice, is to take responsibility for your life and to be in control of your life."
Abbie M. Dale

It is a matter of beginning where you are with yourself. Go after what you think you want in the long run, making moment-to-moment choices based on what feels best with the current options you see for yourself. Rely on your heart with the smaller, less important choices, and gradually you will trust it for the more important decisions.

Your heart is connected to all things within and outside of yourself and can recognize which opportunities are best for you, both immediately and in the long run. To take advantage of your heart's wisdom, you must learn its language and follow its direction.

Exercise

How to discover and acknowledge your desires

1. Before you get out of bed in the morning, ask yourself, "Do I want to get up yet?"

2. If you answer no, stay in bed until you really want to get up. If you answer yes, ask yourself, "Why do I want to get up now?" If you have a reason beyond the "I want to," this is a rational reason, an external motivation, not necessarily a heart desire. Stay in bed until the only reason you have to get up is "I want to."

How does it feel to give in to your desire? Is your day affected in any way? Did you discover anything else about yourself and your desires?

Chapter Three

Learning the Heart's Language

Imagine yourself in your car while stopped at a stop-light. When the light turns green, do you go forward because the light turned green or because you want to go forward? If you go forward only because the light turned green and you know from your driver's manual you are supposed to go on green, you are motivated by an external factor. If you go forward on green because you want to go forward, you are motivated by desire, an internal factor. Most of us drive ahead on a green light because we know we are supposed to and because we want to get where we are going. If you live by

"If you learn to tap into the heart's code, you will be tapping in to the code that is the life force of all systems."

Dr. Paul Pearsall

Heartaculture, you would not move forward until you wanted to.

The "reasoning" of Heartaculture is that the "want to" is a message from the heart. The heart registers everything about you and the world at any given moment and indicates your best choice at that moment by way of your desire or lack of desire for a particular action. It lets you know via the "I want to" what options will most effectively serve your best interests. Your logical mind registers what your eyes see— that the intersection is clear—and then reminds you that a green light means go. Your heart can tell you what your mind can't—that another driver will go through a red light and that if you go forward at that moment you will crash. It does this by way of your desire not to move, or to put it in the positive, your strong desire to stay where you are.

If you are primarily externally motivated, you make most of your conscious choices based on your thought process. You draw from everything you know and logically deduce what options to pick. If you are primarily internally motivated, you make most of your conscious choices based on your feelings. You may logically determine your options, but when making a decision you elect what feels best.

All of us are both externally and internally motivated. We reason out some decisions, while others result from our feelings. In buying a new car we may expend a great deal of energy rationally researching the best make, model and deal. But when it comes to choosing a color, most of us pick a favorite or one that appeals to us at the moment.

When living by Heartaculture you use your rational mind to determine what your options are and then make your decisions with your spiritual mind. You research all your options for a new car and then make your choice, not on what appears to be the best deal, but on which car feels best to you. You may not know why an option feels right but you sum up your feelings with a "want to": This is the car I want.

In the early days of discovering the benefits of Heartaculture, I deliberately tested my "want to's" that went against "reason." One of my first experiments happened spontaneously after drinking a glass of water. I set the empty glass on the kitchen table and started to walk away. Suddenly I felt a strong urge to move the glass and take it to the sink. How odd, I reasoned. What difference could it make? I chose to go against my strong desire to move the glass. I left it where it was, went out of the kitchen and began to go upstairs. At the moment I reached the top stair, I heard a crash downstairs. I immediately ran down to the kitchen and found the glass shattered on the floor.

"Like an ability or a muscle, hearing your inner wisdom is strengthen by doing it."
Robbie Gass

I couldn't imagine who or what had knocked over the glass. I stood there mystified. There was nothing. . . . then suddenly, a gust of wind from the open window behind the table blew the curtains toward me to where the glass had been. The thought that the curtain might knock the glass over had never occurred to me. Instead, something in the subconscious part of myself knew that the glass would be knocked off the table if I left it where it was. I accessed this knowing through my feelings, through my desire to move the glass.

Another experiment I conducted was an ongoing one while I lived in Boston. For my frequent drives to the other side of the city, I determined which route I would take by following my feelings about two possibilities. Each time before starting out, I took a moment to feel what I wanted. I asked myself, Which way do you want to go?

One option, the shortest route, cut through the center of the city and led over the Tobin Bridge. My second option was a route through residential areas that usually took a little longer but was more scenic and pleasant. Sometimes my desire to choose a particular route was quite strong, but at other times I had no real "pull" for either and just picked one. The drive always went without incident. I always arrived easily and safely at my destination.

Since nothing noteworthy was happening to indicate the benefit of one choice over another, I decided to blatantly go against my feelings to see what would happen. One day I had an especially strong desire to take the longer route even though I was leaving later than usual and wanted to make up for lost time. I chose to go against my feelings and took the logical choice, the shorter route, instead. Everything went fine until I got to the expressway around the bridge. Suddenly I was in the middle of one of the worse traffic jams I had ever experienced! It made my drive over an hour longer than usual.

Accessing the Unlimited Spiritual Mind

Your logical mind, much like a computer, can only reason with the information you feed it. This "food" comes from your direct experience and from what you glean from other people's experiences that are shared verbally or visually. Although this accumulated information can be vast, it is limited to the extent of your exposure to the world and is affected by the bias of your conditioning. Your spiritual mind, on the other hand, is not limited to this input. Instead it continuously registers everything that is affecting you in both the physical and spiritual realms. Imagine it as your personal, universal radar detecting your current life-standing at any given moment regardless of your experience, bias, or exposure to the world. Your heart-knowing encompasses far beyond what the logical mind can reason.

In my Boston experiment I logically deduced from my experience that the route through the city over the bridge was the shortest route to my desired destination. I also concluded from my experience and from what I had been taught, that the shortest is usually the quickest. When I was late leaving the house, I rationalized that the shortest route was my best bet for making up time. What I couldn't rationally know was that some traffic mishap would occur along my route. I left early enough to avoid rush hour. Logically then, I would not run into traffic. My desire to take a different route was the feeling-messenger from my spiritual mind. It gave me an up-

> *"The Spirit sees all possibilities. The Will is meant to select what is right for the moment among all possibilities. The Will does this through its feelings."*
>
> *Ceanne DeRohan*

to-the-minute indication that something was occurring in the greater world that would affect my progress. After experiencing the results of my experiment, I logically concluded that next time I would heed my feelings!

You don't need to go to school, read books, know how to use a computer or depend on an outside authority to access the infinite knowing within you. You can access this information merely by recognizing your feelings. This great blessing can also be a handicap. Your ability to make use of your heart-knowing depends on the extent to which you are open and sensitive to your feelings, how you interpret them, and the degree of credibility you attribute to them.

Unfortunately, few of us have been encouraged to acknowledge our feelings, much less credit them with wisdom. We are taught at an early age that our goal is to be rational and logical, rather than feeling and trusting. We are told to "make sense" or "be reasonable" when we are being emotional about an issue, or we are urged to "use common sense" when our desires aren't perceived as rational. Rarely are we asked how we feel about something without also being asked why we feel that way! Why can't it be enough to trust that a feeling is a response to an inner experience and has a validity of its own as a "knowing?" Instead we are asked to rationalize our feelings. In a good percentage of cases, we can comply. We know why we are feeling sad or angry. But what happens when we don't know why we are feeling what we feel?

Have you ever had a strong feeling about someone and couldn't come up with a logical or obvious reason to explain it? This has happened to me on more than one occasion. I discounted my feelings because I couldn't explain them and then wished later that I had given them more credence.

In one case I felt consistently uneasy around the bookkeeper where I worked. She was always pleasant and accommodating but I continued to feel something was "off." Gradually, when nothing surfaced to explain my uneasiness, I pushed my feelings away, even feeling guilty for having them when other people told me how wonderful and capable this woman was. Over a period of time, I accepted my inclination about the bookkeeper as being about me, not her, that there must be something wrong with me if I couldn't feel great about her the way everyone else seemed to. It took a year or so for the truth to emerge. Our cheerful, competent, bookkeeper had skillfully embezzled a small fortune right under our noses!

The imbalance of giving more credence to our rational abilities than to our innate, intuitive capabilities gradually represses our sensitivities to our inner impulses. Little by little we forget to "listen" to ourselves. We no longer pay attention to the voice of our feelings. Instead, we learn to heed the voice of reason, to put more credibility into what we, or someone else, has experienced to be true in the past.

We are taught to deny the feelings that could tell us what is going on in the present.

In retrospect I couldn't help wonder what would have happened if I had trusted my feelings about the bookkeeper and investigated their cause rather than put more validity in my coworkers' opinions. Could I have helped the company detect the embezzlement earlier? I kicked myself for nullifying my feelings, something I was subtly encouraged to do by my mother when I was a child. I would tell her how negatively I was feeling about a classmate or a teacher and she would chastise, "Oh, no, you don't feel that way! She really is a very nice person."

Our feelings are important. They may not all be equal, or indicators of profound truth, but they are the key to accessing our inner selves and our innate knowing about our world, both personal and universal. We do not give enough validity to our feelings because we have been conditioned not to.

To bypass the logical mind and fully access the heart's wisdom takes practice, especially when you are accustomed to doing just the opposite. If you do not ordinarily give credence to your feelings, you may be numb to them or feel uneasy about suddenly acknowledging or trusting them. The beauty of Heartaculture is that you go at your own speed. You begin where you are and slowly develop an intimate relationship with your feelings until acknowledging and trusting them is second nature. Since Heartaculture is about making choices, the feelings you focus on are those that access your heart-knowing about which choices are best for you. Using the shorthand of basic Heartaculture, you focus on

> *"To know what you prefer instead of humbly saying amen to what the world tells you you ought to prefer, is to have kept your soul alive."*
>
> *Robert Louis Stevenson*

your immediate desires. What is it that you want to do, or not do, right now?

Merely asking the question, "Do I want to do this right now?" and answering as honestly as you can in that moment, brings you to a fuller truth about your current reality. Putting your focus on your feelings, if just for a second, begins to etch a clearer pathway to the wisdom of your heart. As you consistently address and acknowledge your present desires, you develop a greater sensitivity to your inner self. Going a step further, deliberately heeding your desires without judging them will evoke a fuller flow to your life force.

Exercise

How to recognize your moment-to-moment desires and allow yourself to follow them

1. Before each activity of your day, ask yourself, "Do I want to do this?" Then ask, "Do I want to do this now?"

2. If you don't want to do something you were about to do, give yourself permission not to do it. Then ask, "What would I rather do?" Give yourself permission to do that instead.

3. Keep the action you decide not to do immediately as an option for another time during the day. Do it only if and when you want to do it.

4. Pay attention to your feelings as you follow your desires rather than the "shoulds." If you go against a desire and give into a "should," notice how you feel and what happens as a result.

Chapter Four

Respecting Your Desires

Perhaps the hardest part of following Heartaculture is learning not to label what you think you want as "right" or "wrong." When you first begin to give yourself permission to do only what you want to do, and not do anything you don't want to do, you may experience a strong sense of doing something improper. Deeply ingrained "shoulds" can make it difficult to consider "want to's" before taking care of supposed obligations. Much like a child who gobbles down dessert before eating his dinner, doing what you would like to do instead of doing what you think is expected may make you feel downright rebellious. Understandably so!

"I don't know the key to success, but the key to failure is trying to please everybody."

Bill Cosby

Our conditioning about what is "right" and what is "wrong" begins the day we are born. As infants and children, we learn to adapt our behaviors according to the responses we receive from our environment. Gradually, as we grow from children to adults, we discover which of our behaviors bring favorable responses and meet our desires, and which bring disapproval and perhaps punishment.

If you eat everything on your plate, you get dessert.

If you clean your room, you can go to the movies with your friends.

If you get an "F" on your report card, you can't go to summer camp.

We learn that when we obey or please the authorities in our lives we are considered "good." When we are "good" we get what we want. Our authorities include our parents, teachers, friends, peers, bosses, partners, doctors, religious leaders, scientists, and government officials, or anyone we look to for direction, approval or sanction.

"Good" and "right" become equivalent when we do whatever our authorities think is good and we are considered "right" for doing so. Or, vice versa, we do what our authorities think is right and we are considered "good" when we do. If the priest says it is good to go to confession, we are doing "right" when we go and feel guilty when we don't. It is "right" to go to college, but if we choose not to go, we aren't quite as "good" as the people who do go.

From experience we discover it is best to do what is "right" because then we reap the rewards given to good children, good students, good employees, good spouses and good citizens. We get the approval and acceptance we want. To do otherwise, to go against what our authorities want us to do, brings scorn, punishment, exclusion, or ridicule. Taking extra long lunch hours at work earns dirty looks or reprimands by fellow employees or the boss. We are "wrong" or "bad" when failing to file our tax returns on time, and we are penalized. We are laughed at when we wear plaids and stripes together because our peers consider it unfashionable.

As a child you learned how to brush your teeth, but did you want to brush them every day? Most children don't naturally correlate brushing regularly with healthy teeth and gums. More likely you brushed after meals or at bedtime because your parents insisted on it. Gradually, you learned to want to brush your teeth because your parents would say things like, "As soon as you brush your teeth, I'll read you a story," or "Good girl!" when they inspected your gleaming mouth. Little by little we are conditioned to want what our authorities want for us.

"Freedom is that instant between when someone tells you to do something and when you decide how to respond."

Dr. Jeffrey Borenstein

A substantial part of growing up is learning which choices are considered right or wrong, good or bad, by our authorities. We use these pronouncements to prompt our choices for everything, from when to get up, what to eat, how to dress, where to go, how to go, and what to accomplish on any given day. We learn to want to do the "right" things because we like the acceptance, privileges and paybacks we get as rewards.

Accepting direction from our elders or people who have more knowledge than we do can be very practical and smart. We learn by the experience of others so we don't have to discover or reinvent everything on our own. Much of our early conditioning provides valuable structure and direction to our fledgling existence until we are ready to manage our own destinies. Unfortunately, after years of learning to follow a program designed by others, we forget to check-in with ourselves to see if the "right" we acquired through our conditioning is best for us as individuals.

The Influence of Conditioning

Our conditioned compliance to childhood authorities is echoed in the choices we make in our adulthood. As children we did as we were told to get what we wanted and to be treated nicely, or at least left alone and not punished. If we followed the rules (written or implied) at school, our days went more smoothly and we were given higher grades than if we talked during class or turned in our homework late. As adults, we try to fit in at work, follow the dress code (explicit or implied), watch the clock for our arrivals and departures, accomplish our work as we have been directed, and learn to "market" ourselves according to what we think is expected or wanted from us.

The voices of our earliest authorities continue to dictate the rightness or wrongness of our wants and choices without our suspecting they are an influence. If you like to read in bed before falling asleep, perhaps you can relate to my experience. Sometimes I'm too sleepy and too comfortable to get out of bed to brush my teeth before turning the lights out. I spend several minutes deliberating whether I "should" get up, or could I just this once skip brushing my teeth before sleeping. It is a real dilemma! I want to stay in bed, but I know I should want to brush my teeth. After all, I DO WANT the healthy teeth I've been taught come with brushing. But I DON'T WANT to get up! I wish I had brushed my teeth before getting into bed, but I didn't. So what do I do? Sometimes I drag myself reluctantly to the bathroom to brush, and maybe even floss, and feel very "good" (Good girl, Ellen) when I get back into bed. I fall asleep with a clear conscience. Other times, I say, FORGET IT! I am NOT getting up! I feel very mutinous as I quickly flip the light switch and plop my head down on the pillow. In the morning I accept the awful fuzzy feeling in my mouth as the deserved consequence of my rebellion. Some part of me feels I've done something wrong, even when I reason that missing a brushing once or twice (or even thrice) won't make my teeth rot.

Over time the practice of making choices based on the subtle or blatant approval or disapproval of our authorities forces our true desires to recede under layers of programmed responses. To get to the truth of our hearts, we need to ask ourselves if what we think we want is what we really want. Even when we answer this question as honestly as we can, it may still take repeated asking to evoke the true answer. What we think we want is often what we think we should want. We want what we should want because it is what our authorities tell us is good, and therefore right, to want. We act on these "shoulds" without comparing our thinking with our feelings. Automatically we assume that what is right to do is what we want to do.

> *"No one can make you feel inferior without your consent."*
>
> *Eleanor Roosevelt*

I am going to mow the lawn now.

Do I really want to mow the lawn?

Yes, I should mow the lawn.

Do I really want to mow the lawn?

Yes, I need to mow the lawn.

Do I really want to mow the lawn now?

Well, I'd rather play golf.

Imagine yourself in this situation: You are in bed and your baby crying in another room awakens you. It is your job to take care of the baby, but you do not want to get out of bed. Are you wrong for wanting to stay in bed and not wanting to jump right out of bed to get the baby? Most likely your conditioning makes you wrong. How could you be so heartless? Your poor, helpless child depends on you. Guilt, guilt, guilt!

We judge ourselves negatively for wanting something other than what we learned we should want. This judgment is a conditioned subconscious response. Even after years of successfully negotiating adulthood, we automatically feel we are doing something wrong when we consider doing what we want to do before, or instead of, doing what we think we should do. The "should" is a voice in our heads from a parent or other "authority." The authority is often the general unofficial consensus of the society in which we live.

I have clients who tell me they feel wrong about wanting to be rich when they are already making a good-enough income, or they feel guilty about wanting time for themselves away from their families. They think the desire to be rich is being greedy, that they should be satisfied and thankful for what they have, that taking time for themselves is selfish or irresponsible. You are not supposed to want things for yourself, right? Rather, we are conditioned to provide for others first before we give to ourselves. We are so accustomed to living by our "shoulds" that we feel guilty or "bad" when we discover that what we want isn't what we should want.

The Limiting Effects of Judging Desires

Labeling what you want as good, bad, right or wrong, keeps you from discovering your true desires, limits your options and affects the quality of your life. If you consider it "bad" to want to cancel a scheduled evening with friends at the last minute, you will find it difficult to consider other options. You may prefer to stay home to get some badly needed rest, or go to the movies with your children. Going out with your friends when you do not want to go may make you feel resentful for "having to go" and thus negatively affect the quality of the evening. If you consider it "good" to want to do for others before doing for yourself, you may never consider your real desires or needs and end up depending on others to take care of you. If you feel it is "wrong" to want to say no to the demands of your boss, you may get a raise, but you may also work twice as hard and longer hours than you are getting paid for. Over a period of time, working more than you want will affect your attitude toward your job and yourself. It will also affect the quality of your life. If you are spending

> *"The first step to getting the things you want out of life is this: Decide what you want."*
>
> Ben Stein

all your time working, you won't have time or energy to do other things you prefer doing. If you think it is "right" to want to spend every weekend with your spouse, you may never consider enrolling in a weekend writing workshop to discover your talent as a novelist.

When you make a judgment about what you think you want or don't want, what you are saying is "I should," or "I shouldn't—."

Wanting to stay home instead of going out with my friends is selfish.

(I should be with my friends tonight because I told them I would be.)

It is terrible that I want to watch TV when it is time to make dinner for the family.

(I should do for others before doing for myself.)

I am wrong for not wanting to work overtime.

(I shouldn't say no to my boss.)

Choosing to go hiking with my friend on Saturday is disloyal.

(I should spend every weekend with my spouse.)

As young children we did not judge our wants. "Shoulds" and "shouldn'ts" are learned judgments. We pick them up from the authorities in our lives, from external sources. They come with the conditioned belief that being "good" or doing what is "right" is the best way to reap desired rewards.

Eliminating these deeply ingrained conditioned responses is not easy when a good/bad/, right/wrong rationale is predominant in our society. Our public schools, laws and social codes all encourage going along with the program. It is difficult to go against what you are immersed in. It is like trying to stop smoking amid nicotine addicts. Other people may see the worth of your resolve but there is little support in the way of mentoring or infrastructure.

Becoming the Authority in Your Life

When you ask yourself if what you have planned for your day is what you want to do, you are taking the first step toward freeing yourself from constricting conditioning and discovering your true heart. The trick is to stop running on automatic pilot and begin making conscious moment-to-moment choices about how you want your life to be. After you ask yourself, "Is this what I want to do right now?" give yourself full permission to do, or not do what you want or don't want to do, even if you find yourself saying, "I shouldn't" or "I should."

When you ask yourself, "What do I want to do?" accept your answer without judgment. Do not label it. If it is what you feel you want, don't put yourself down or praise yourself for wanting it.

"I'm really selfish. I want to stay home and read instead of going with my husband to the football game."

"I want to volunteer at the nursing home. Isn't that great?"

Instead, see your desire as a perfectly fine option and nothing else. Stay neutral. Erase any thoughts of being good, bad, right or wrong for wanting what you want. Just as you wouldn't judge a child for wanting candy, don't judge yourself for your desires.

Once you eliminate these judgments and acknowledge the unconditional validity of your desires, your increased options will help you to be freer, lighter, and more creative. When anything you want becomes an option, your world of possibilities expands immensely. If you no longer automatically accept the prejudice from outer authorities about your desires, you can consider what you think you want more authentically.

> *"Some men have thousands of reasons why they cannot do what they want to, when all they need is one reason why they can."*
> *Mary Frances Berry*

Bypassing the outer voices and creating a neutral frame of mind allows you to more easily feel your heart and know whether your desire is what you want to pursue or not.

When you give yourself permission to consider all options as valid, you empower yourself as *the* authority in your life. You open yourself to options you never thought possible when you were concerned about pleasing some outer authority. When you are your own authority, you can please yourself. (No matter how selfish or bad that sounds or feels!) By empowering yourself as the "in-house" authority, you make a transition from being externally motivated—encouraged to do something by factors outside yourself—to being internally motivated, moved to act by factors within yourself. You can then choose to act on the desires that more directly and currently express who you are. These desires are "dearer" to your heart.

This transference of power enlivens your life force. It stirs your creativity. When you take the lid off the suppressed expression of your desires, hope blazes. The possibility of expressing your true heart quickens your spirit and gives you energy. Once you open to this expanded realm of possibilities, you can begin correlating your desires with your deeper feelings to determine if what you think you want is what you really want.

Collapsing the Walls of Limitation

When you give yourself full permission to do what you want to do, the walls of limitation collapse. Feel what it is like to suddenly remove the ban or judgment on something that you previously perceived as right or wrong, good or bad. Your unconditional acceptance of your desire as a potential option momentarily suspends any consideration of morality or duty. Depending on where you are with yourself, this sudden release of all bonds to external authorities can be exhilarating or frightening.

No matter how freeing, this new experience of being the authority in your life can cause momentary confusion. It is similar to being released from prison after thirty years of incarceration. It can be disorientating to put aside a structure that dictated your choices for so long. Suppressed desires surface, pressing to be satisfied. These are often derivatives of true desires, shaped by hurt, anger, and deprivation and charged with emotions that are hard to sort out.

A Trappist monk friend of mine who had entered a monastery in his teens chose to leave his celibate life at age fifty. Soon after he experienced sex for the first time, he confessed he was afraid he would become a pervert. He was obsessed with thoughts and desire for sex and experienced a roller coaster of emotions ranging from joy and relief to anger and guilt. I assured him his obsession was normal under the circumstances and to give himself time to come into the present with himself. As he gave into his preoccupation without judgment, he quickly satiated himself and developed a healthy sex life.

> *"Self-reliance is the only road to true freedom, and being one's own person is its ultimate reward."*
>
> *Patricia Sampson*

A man crossing the desert without water to drink can suppress his desire to drink knowing there is no water available. The desire to drink is still there, prompted by a basic biological need for fluid, but he can't act on it. As soon as he sees water and knows drinking is an option, his desire to drink becomes a craving and preoccupation. When he reaches the water, he immediately drinks as much as he can—which may be well beyond his need.

As you ban the "shoulds" and "shouldn'ts" in your life and your suppressed desires emerge, you may experience strong yearnings that need to be recognized without judgment. When considering the steps to fulfill these longings, mixed emotions may make it difficult to discern what you are feeling. It may be hard to recognize whether what you think you want is what you really want. At these times it is especially important to check in with your internal heart-will indicators. These physical perceptions, discerned from emotions, indicate what is best for you (on all levels) in the present.

Imagine a rejected lover who, in the throws of his emotions, runs to the edge of a cliff with the intention of jumping over. The impetus of his emotions may be enough to cause him to jump. If, however, he stops for a moment and asks himself, "Do I really want to do this?" he allows himself to get in touch with the truth of his heart. If his answer is, "Oh my, no! I may kill myself!" he is answering from reason. If he answers, "I feel like I want to die, but to jump doesn't feel right," he has attuned to his heart.

Exercise

How to empower yourself as the authority in your life

1. Eliminate the words "should" and "shouldn't" from your vocabulary. When you find yourself saying or thinking "I should" or "I shouldn't," stop and correct yourself by saying "I want to" or "I don't want to."

Example

Instead of "I should call my sister," say, "I want to call my sister."

Instead of "I shouldn't spend my money on a new car," say, "I don't want to spend my money on a new car."

2. Notice how you feel when you make this switch. The ball is fully in your court when you eliminate the outside authority, real or imagined, that created the "should" or "shouldn't." Then you can decide whether you really want to do whatever it is or not.

You may find that you don't want to do the "should," or that you do want to do the "shouldn't," or vice versa. What matters is that you remove the judgment and make an authentic, internally motivated choice.

Chapter Five

Fine Tuning to the Heart's Knowing

When you assume full responsibility for determining what options you have, you need to determine whether or not these options are in keeping with your greatest good. Your greatest good is that which is most beneficial for you in fulfilling your potential. This applies both to the endeavors for which you strive and to your overall well-being on all levels. When making a choice, use your rational mind to list all the options you want to consider. Then pick the one or ones that you think you want to do. The next step is to determine if what you think you want to do is in keeping with what your heart wants.

"In the important decisions of personal life, we should be governed, I think, by the deep inner needs of our nature."

Sigmund Freud

To decipher the deeper knowing of the heart in order to make internal choices, there is a skill that is especially beneficial to develop. This is being able to discern the feelings in the body that are the internal indicators of your heart-will. Some part of you knows what is going on in the world at every moment. Your body holds this knowing. It can indicate when an action is advantageous or not in the short or long run. Everyone has the ability to perceive these signals, but it takes focus and practice to feel confident about acting on them.

Before you proceed with this paragraph, ask yourself, "Am I warm enough right now?" Or perhaps, "Am I too warm?" Take a few seconds to feel if you are comfortable. For you to answer this question, you need to attune to your physical self. You are either comfortable or not. This is the same process you use to know if an option feels good or not. As you hold the thought in your mind of the option you are considering, feel your body. Not only can you feel if you are comfortable temperature-wise, you can feel if you are generally comfortable and at rest, or peaceful, on a deeper level.

As you practice paying attention to your body while making choices, you will learn which physical feelings are the green light, the go-ahead indicators of the heart, and which are the red light, the wait indicators. Sometimes the signals are blatant: a sense of heaviness or foreboding, a strong pulling in one direction or another, or a bubbly, excited sensation. Most times, however, the feelings are subtler: a closed, shutdown, or "I don't want to move" feeling that indicates "No, do not take this action now." Or you may experience an open, "I want to go" feeling, a yes, indicating the action would be appropriate.

When you focus on the choice you are considering, you can feel by these physical indicators if your deeper self is in agreement with this choice or if you need to modify the option. For example, perhaps you are considering walking out to the mailbox to pick up your mail, hoping your tax return has arrived. In your mind you think this is what you would like to do. Now feel your body. Does it seem ready to go? Or do you feel "neutral" or a lackluster feeling? If you feel a positive, yes feeling physically, or a strong pull to go to the mailbox, it is most likely that either your tax return or some other mail that you will be happy to have has arrived. If you feel a lack of energy for going to the mailbox, there is most likely nothing of interest for you in the mailbox, possibly no mail at all. In either case, check the mailbox to see if you are interpreting your indicators correctly. During your day's activities experiment with little tests similar to this to see how your indicators function.

> *"Every time you don't follow your inner guidance, you feel a loss of energy, loss of power, a sense of spiritual deadness."*
>
> *Shakti Gawain*

Perusing your internal indicators will tell you in any one moment what is most advantageous for you. It is a simple way to stay continuously connected to your innate or intuitive knowing. This attunement to your world can be very practical and efficient, often saving you unnecessary steps.

This is a tool I use constantly. I have plenty of opportunity to test its practicality in the life I lead in a secluded canyon in Arizona where there are no telephone lines. I have considered using a pager or cell phone, but have opted instead to keep my innate skills honed by relying on them exclusively.

In the morning when I am considering my options for the day, I list all the things I think I want to accomplish. Then, as I run down the list, I ask myself which option I want to do first. If one option "jumps" out at me with a strong green-light body sensation, I decide to do that first. If I don't have a strong preference for any of the options, I briefly feel each option separately.

The sensations in my body let me know when there is a "charge" on the option, indicating I need to pay attention. Considering this option, I ask, "Do I want to do this now?" and I sense my body for red or green-light indicators. It may be a report to write, a phone call to make, a housekeeping task to do. The option with the strongest positive charge is the one I do first. If all the options feel about equal, I just pick one and begin to do it.

Intermittently during the day I stop what I'm doing and ask myself if I want to continue with what I'm focused on, or switch to something else. As I mentally go through my options, I feel which one feels the best and either continue with my current activity or shift to another depending on my desire and physical indicators. When I proceed with the day in this manner, things flow easily with synchronicity. I accomplish much more and experience more enjoyment than when I force myself to do something that I tell myself has to get done now. Seeming "procrastination" does have its purpose!

With one particular aspect of my day, timing is especially important. It has to do with deciding when to retrieve messages from the phone at my office, which is located a mile away. I gauge how soon I need to go to the phone by the tension or lack of tension I feel physically when I ask myself if I want to go to the phone now. If I do want to go to the phone and feel a strong physical pull as well, I know I need to go right away. If I don't have a strong desire to go to the phone right then, I decide not to go. If I don't feel a tension, or pull, I know there won't be messages I need to respond to immediately.

Sometimes when I am at my computer, deeply engrossed in what I am writing, I suddenly become aware that I feel restless. I stop and ask, "What do I want to do now?" The answer is often "I want to go to my office." Invariably when I get this answer, I have an important message that needs immediate attention, or a call from the person I've been waiting to hear from. Occasionally, I feel a strong pull to hurry to the phone, and when I heed this inclination, the phone is often ringing as I enter my office, and the person I've wanted to talk to is on the line.

> *"There is a coherent plan in the universe, though I don't know what it's a plan for."*
>
> *Fred Hoyle*

To test this way of knowing when there are time-sensitive messages I need to respond to, I have gone to the phone purposely when I have not felt a desire or physical pull to do so. There are either no messages at all or only informative messages that I don't need to respond to immediately. When I rely on this system for message retrieval, I save time by not going to my phone needlessly.

Trusting Your Physical Indicators

As attuning to your body becomes routine, you will become more sensitive to what it is telling you. Your physical indicators will make themselves "heard" when you need to pay attention to what you are or are not doing. Occasionally when you are about to do something, you will begin to feel uneasy, or some part of you, your stomach, for example, will tense up. If you have ever experienced the sense that you have forgotten something just as you are leaving the house to go somewhere, you have felt what I am talking about. Another common experience is to be lost and feel that going in one direction feels better than going in another. You may experience this as a physical pulling to the right or left, or perhaps a very heavy "no" sensation when you begin to move in the wrong direction.

When you acknowledge that you are feeling uncomfortable physically while considering an option, give yourself permission not to do whatever it is. In fact, decide not to do it. If the uncomfortable feeling eases with your decision, you know not to proceed with the action at that point. Sometimes, however, a new tension is created when when you consider not doing an action. For example, imagine preparing to give a speech in front of a large audience. You notice you are feeling uncomfortable physically, especially in your stomach. When you give yourself permission not to give the speech, the tension in your stomach lets up, but a new, more general tension develops. The new option—not giving the speech —makes your body feel "closed." When you decide you will not give the speech, you feel heavy. But then if you decide to go ahead with the speech, see if the heaviness lifts and if your body feels "open." If it does, you know giving the speech would be a good thing to do and the feeling in your stomach is most likely performance anxiety.

When considering what your body is telling you, you may not feel anything distinctive. It could be that you are numbed to your feelings from habitually ignoring them, or it could be that the action you are considering is not important in the larger scheme of things. A neutral feeling usually indicates an insignificant action, one that doesn't necessarily lead toward, or keep you from, fulfilling your potential. For example, you may ask what color socks you want to wear. You decide you prefer blue and check in with your body to see how your decision feels. Your body may feel "open," so you know that blue socks are fine, but there is no big pull in one direction to wear or not to wear them. You may test by deciding not to wear them and see if your body indicators change. If they don't, you will know it doesn't matter one way or another.

As you get into the routine of first asking, "Is this what I want to do right now" and then checking how you feel physically before taking action, your heart-will indicators become more apparent. It is really your attention that is changing. You notice the sensations in your body more readily because your attention is automatically attuned. Gradually, you will become simultaneously aware of your internal indicators with your choices: As soon as you consider an option, the feelings will be instantly obvious without having to ask yourself how you feel.

As you learn to trust your choices based on your desires and your physical indicators, notice how the "coincidences" in your life increase. Possibly spontaneously you will want to dine at a restaurant you rarely go to, and it is there that you bump into a long lost friend. Or maybe your boss will want you to go to a meeting that you absolutely do not want to go to, and for no particular reason, the meeting is cancelled. Coincidence? Your strong desire or negative response to any option is a message from your heart-knowing about what is going on in the world.

Occasionally I have a strong red-light body reaction to a potential client who calls to make an appointment. Since the person is new to me, there is no rational reason why I wouldn't want to see them. My aversion to making an appointment is so strong I struggle with myself not to make some excuse to say that I can't see them. Over the years I have learned to go ahead and make the appointment, despite my misgivings, because it won't happen anyway. The client always calls and cancels. I have learned what this body reaction means and have come to trust it.

The tendency is to rationalize our feelings. Perhaps this is a way to talk ourselves out of having the feelings so we can ignore them. We feel we shouldn't have objections to something that logically seems good for us.

"Trying On" Your Options

Imagine having tickets to a special concert. On the night of the event, you suddenly have no desire to go. The thought of curling up in bed with a good book is very appealing. You rationalize that you are tired from working all day, and the thought of driving the distance to the concert is probably why you don't want to go. Then you think of the expense of the tickets and how you were really looking forward to the concert. You tell yourself that once you are there you will be glad you went. You can't decide whether to push yourself to go or to stay home. This is a time to attune to your physical indicators.

First, tell yourself that either option is equally permissible. It is okay to go to the concert and it is okay to stay home. Then close your eyes and consciously clear your mind for a moment. Put yourself into a neutral mental place by imagining your mind as a blank TV screen. Take a deep breath and relax. Then, action by action, imagine how it would be to go to the concert. Feel how it feels to get dressed, go out of the house, get in the car, drive to the theater, park, walk into the theater, sit down and listen to the concert. Can you feel each step? Sum up how the experience feels with a word or two. Then imagine yourself staying home and how that feels. Which option feels best when you "try it on"?

If your mind begins making up reasons for your feelings, try again. Totally feel your body, instead of thinking how it feels. If this is difficult to do, take another deep breath or two, sink further into your body and relax. Ask yourself if you are warm enough. Once you sense your physical temperature, you are attuned to your body and can go from there. Compare how the options feel when you imagine doing them. When your mind is in conflict, your internal indicators will give you your answer for which option is best.

It is often only in retrospect that the reason for one option feeling better than another option becomes clear. If, as in the concert example, you feel staying home is best, you might discover the next day that the concert was cancelled at the last moment due to the sudden illness of the performer. (That happened to me!) Or maybe you will get an important phone call that you would have missed if you weren't home. It is by experience and paying attention that you learn what your body's signals are and their significance. When you see how they can save you time and stress, or perhaps keep you safe, you will learn to heed them.

A friend of mine who lives by Heartaculture had this experience. She had a meeting to go to in another city, which was over ninety miles away. Her teenage son decided to drive with her so they could do something special together after the meeting. They were on their way when after twenty minutes my friend suddenly realized she didn't want to go on. She asked her son how he felt. He, too, said he no longer wanted to go. They both felt a strong physical aversion to proceeding. Instead of talking herself out of the feeling by rationalizing how important the meeting was, my friend turned the car around and headed home. Both she and her son felt relieved. It was only the next day that she realized why she had had the change of heart. She read in the newspaper that there was a drive-by shooting on the highway she would have taken to get to the meeting. She calculated that if she had proceeded as planned, she would have been exactly where the incident occurred at the time it happened.

Through relying on your desires and body indicators over time, you will learn to relax and trust these inner authorities rather than your outer authorities. You will begin to trust your heart thinking more than your mind thinking. Giving credence to your desires and physical indicators, moment by moment, pays off by helping you live "in the flow." You will be more relaxed in usually stressful situations and find that more often than not you are in the right place at the most opportune or appropriate time.

Exercise 1

How do your internal indicators "speak" to you?

1. Take a deck of playing cards. Separate out three pairs. Example: a pair of aces, a pair of threes and a pair of sixes. Suit does not matter. (Alternative: Use six identical objects such as poker chips or index cards instead of playing cards. Mark the objects on one side to have three pairs of numbers. One way is to write numbers on pieces of masking tape and fasten one to each of the objects.)

2. Place the six cards face down and scramble them to be sure you do not remember the position of specific numbers.

3. Pick one card. Look at the number and put the card aside.

4. Now ask, "Where is the pair to this one?" Hold your hand flat over the cards that are face down.

5. As you pass your hand over the cards, sense which card wants to come to you or which card feels different than the others.

6. Turn over the card that you have a sense about. See if it is a pair to the first card you picked.

The process is the important part of this exercise. Do not get discouraged if you are unable to match the card correctly at first. The point is to become sensitive to the messages your heart is giving you. Repeat the exercise until you sense your internal indicators. Repeating the exercise several times in quick succession can help emphasize your perceptions. Once you are confident that you feel your indicators, you can hone your interpretation by practicing for accuracy. Keep the cards handy and repeat the exercise in spare moments during your day.

Exercise 2

1. Before you make a phone call, ask, "Will the person I am calling be available?" What do your internal indicators tell you? Do you feel a red light or a green light, a yes or no? Perhaps a good feeling means yes, or a "flat" or neutral feeling means no.

2. Make the call. Did you interpret your internal indicators correctly? It may take practice before you decipher accurately.

Chapter Six

Heart–Time Versus Clock Time

Perhaps the hardest external authority to disregard is the clock. Being "on time," a virtue we strive to live up to, will take on new meaning as you discover the advantages of the heart's timing. Your heart really does know best, even when your "responsible" brain tells you your heart doesn't know what it is "talking" about!

Our hearts are constantly updating us about the conditions in the world around us. If we follow them we will be led to the places (both physically and spiritually) where we need to be at the most advantageous time. When we allow our hearts to determine the what and the

"It's not enough to be busy—so are the ants. The question is: What are we busy about?"

Henry David Thoreau

when of our actions, we allow the synchronicity of the universe to best support us in the greater scheme of achieving our destinies and full potential.

It can be difficult to reprogram yourself to slow down enough to feel the pacing your heart urges you to follow. Oddly enough, by slowing down you can often accomplish more with less effort.

You may have experienced the truth of this if you have ever driven in several lanes of traffic while hurrying to get somewhere. To make headway you switch lanes back and forth, weaving around the slower cars until finally you break out in front and zip ahead at your own pace unimpeded. But what is that? A stoplight! Being ahead of everyone else, you are the first to stop! In humility you watch as all the other cars you worked so hard to pass come to stand beside you at the stoplight, the great leveler in the motorist world. To your further chagrin, the light turns green and the car you passed minutes before comes sailing through in the "slow" lane without needing to stop. It is the old tortoise and hare adage. Chronic running and pushing ahead does not necessarily advance you faster than anyone else nor will it necessarily accomplish your goals faster or more efficiently and effectively.

When you are racing around meeting "deadlines," you often bypass the support the universe can offer. You may be so committed to the actions you have chosen to do that you do not allow yourself to stray from your chosen course in spite of what you may rather want to do. Your brain tells you to stay on track or you will not accomplish what you need to "on time." On the other hand, being flexible by using your original plan as a guide and spontaneously deviating as your heart indicates will help you obtain the best possible results in the most effective and effortless manner. Timing is crucial. By waiting to complete a task until you are internally motivated, you wait until all elements are in the most opportune position. You will use less energy and effort to create a desired outcome "in the flow" of heart-will than if you force actions that are part of a "logical" plan.

The downside at times, if you choose to see it this way, is that by following heart-time you may not always accomplish what you set out to do by the deadline you originally chose to follow. Clock time may seem to get you the results you desire in the short run, but heart-time results will be the most beneficial to you in the long term. **The way of Heartaculture is to keep an eye on the future, on where you want to be, but to act in the present by doing what feels best.**

By following your internal timing, by doing what feels best step-by-step, you adjust yourself gradually to heart or universal time. You know when you have arrived when your days flow well, with everything fitting together with minimal effort and frequent "coincidences."

Living in the canyon without a telephone, I rely on my internal authority to alert me to circumstances beyond my immediate environment that may affect the timing of actions in a plan I have chosen to follow. For example, when I invite someone for dinner for the following weekend, I make up the menu and schedule the day I will shop at the nearest supermarket, which is thirty miles away. On the day scheduled I check with myself to feel if I want to go shopping. When the answer is no, I

> *"When, in a given situation, the time is not ripe for further progress, the best thing to do is to wait quietly, without ulterior designs. If one acts thoughtlessly and tries to push ahead in opposition to fate, success will not be achieved."*
>
> *I Ching*

give myself permission not to go. I then consider my options: 1) change the menu to use the ingredients I have on hand, 2) go shopping on a different day, or 3) take my guest to the local café for dinner.

On two specific occasions when I expected company for dinner, I chose not to shop at all. When the time came for cooking the meal to have it ready when my guests arrived, I didn't feel like cooking and gave myself permission not to. On the first occasion I expected my guests to come for dinner and stay overnight. When they didn't arrive even an hour after they were due, I went ahead and did what I felt like doing. I prepared something simple for myself to eat and then read a book. When my visitors eventually did arrive, hours later, they had already eaten. On the second occasion my two guests arrived on time but said they didn't want anything to eat—they were fasting!

By heeding my desires on both occasions, I saved myself the trips to town to shop and the needless preparation of meals that wouldn't be eaten. Since I did only what I wanted to do, I didn't resent my guests for not wanting dinner. I could fully relax and enjoy the evening. Heeding my feelings about not wanting to shop or cook, I remained attuned to the universe and saved myself stress and needless effort while achieving my purpose to please and enjoy my guests.

To arrive at this point of confidence in heart-timing versus clock time took many years of taking chances and observing the results. Believe me I have not always been so relaxed! My old mode of forcing myself to accomplish all the tasks I set up for myself by my self-imposed deadlines, no matter what interruptions or hurdles I encountered, resulted in late nights, frazzled nerves, and being irritable and exhausted. Realizing I did not enjoy this process motivated me to experiment with a different way.

Deadlines have very little to do with the timing of events in our greater world unless they are made with the heart involved. To be our most productive and efficient selves, waiting until everything feels right before taking action makes sense. At times this may look like procrastination and it is. You are putting off what doesn't feel right and waiting for the time your actions will be more effective. In the long run, you save time, energy, and possibly money. Often if you wait to do things when you want to do them, you will find a much simpler solution to accomplishing what you had in mind. Recently I put off washing my very muddy car because I didn't feel like doing it. After a week or so, I was driving home and realized it was time; I was ready to wash it. When I turned off the highway onto my road, a handmade sign indicated a charity car wash. I followed the arrow and found the local firemen washing cars to raise money for needy families at Christmas. They cleaned my car for a donation in half the time it would have taken me. Additionally, I felt good about contributing to benefit others.

> *"You can be sure that when the season is right, your desires will manifest. This is the Law of Least Effort."*
>
> *Deepak Chopra*

Trusting Heart-Time

The Heartaculture approach to timing takes resolve and trust, especially at first. As you complete tasks only when you are internally motivated, you may need determination to tune out urgings to "hurry" or follow a specified order of actions. With a fast-paced world conducting its business according to the clock, it is hard not to get caught up in the frenetic activity to accomplish everything "on time." When the people around you, perhaps your boss, fellow workers, or your family members, are in their heads about when and how things should be done, you need to trust your own pacing. Who creates deadlines anyway? Often in the case of business (busy-ness) it is the material whip that cracks over our heads. Onward! The faster we get things done, the quicker we can make more money.

Unfortunately, not all the people you feel subordinate to at work, home, or school will patiently watch you operate in Heartaculture mode. If you can do it quietly, maybe they won't notice! If they do follow your process, however, they could express their fear about anticipated consequences if results aren't forthcoming at the designated time. They may criticize your methods, accuse you of procrastination, or demand you do it their way. Guard against their fear becoming your fear. If you do give in to their demands, make the choice consciously and watch the results of each step you take. Are you able to complete the task easily, or are you constantly running into frustrations or stoplights?

Perhaps you are organizing an event for a specific date. A typical approach to having a successful result is to establish a timeline by which tasks need to be completed. This is a good start. Then as you scan your timeline, pick the tasks and their timing by what you want to do when you want to do it. Use your body indicators to confirm your timing. What feels right to you may not "think" right to other more rational committee members. But stick to your guns! While they are frantically making phone calls, and often after several tries not connecting with the people they need to talk to, you make each of your calls only once, connecting with the right person immediately or catching them in the perfect mood to grant your request.

It may look like fellow workers are accomplishing more than you by their rush-rush approach, but hang in there. Often the arrangements made by the rational approach fall through or have to be readjusted several times before they stick. Relax, hold the final deadline for the event in mind, but don't watch the calendar or clock as you complete each task on the list in heart-time. You will find that by not worrying along the way about the deadline, you will often finish your tasks well before the anticipated timeline without the usual stress.

When choosing dates and times for future meetings, appointments, trips, and completing tasks, check in with your body indicators. When you feel the go-ahead signs that indicate the schedule you are considering is in alignment with your best good, you are most apt to have an advantageous "flow" on those days and times for whatever it is you are wanting to do.

When two or more people are involved in picking a date, choose one that feels good to everyone. This will give you a better chance for having a produc-tive time without hitches than when you pick times that people object to but compromise and agree to any-way. When a date is picked far ahead of the actual event and involves a large number of people,

"Calendars are for careful people, not passionate ones."

Chuck Weblog

the date must feel good to the planners. This feeling good sums up the heart's knowing what will produce the best out-come for the intended purpose of the event and for everyone involved. When the actual day or time for the event arrives, some people, for one reason or another, may not be able to attend. Although these people thought they wanted to par-ticipate, on a deeper level they had a more pressing agenda.

When events have a predetermined schedule, say the fourth Saturday of every month, these dates may or may not all be the most advantageous for producing effective outcomes. Thus it is best to be flexible. The ideal would be to use the predetermined schedule as a guide, but adjust the dates individually to what feels good to the group or powers that be.

Of course, in the extremely scheduled world we have today, if everyone started to adjust predetermined schedules at the same time, we would have total chaos, at least at first. If heart-time eventually prevailed, however, it would have an order of its own. When I have observed groups of people consciously using heart-time, the order is one of relaxed synchronicity.

Eliminating Stress

When you are able to be internally motivated for each step in a process, you will find how much more easily you can complete tasks with the desired result. It may be so easy that you fear you have not really completed the task, or that you have forgotten something. Once you have experienced the simplicity of accomplishing tasks by following your inner authority, your trust, and possibly the trust of your family or co-workers, will grow stronger.

Using heart-time for work or personal matters will eventually help you eliminate a great deal of stress. In the beginning, however, while learning to trust, you may find yourself dealing with more stress! Your fear that following your heart won't work and may lead you into trouble creates the stress. The only remedy I know for this is to try heart-time first for less significant matters to acquire experience and then build up to more "risky" experiments.

After several years of living by Heartaculture in my personal life, I gained enough trust to use it in my work life as well. At a new job as assistant director of a small private elementary school, I was in charge of public relations. The fall semester had just begun when the director requested that I interview a newly hired teacher and write a press release for the local paper announcing the appointment. As a writer, I happily agreed to the assignment. Each day, however, when I decided my agenda according to what felt best to me, I kept putting off interviewing the new teacher. After a week the director asked me if I had written the story yet. Another week passed and when she asked again, I still hadn't completed the interview. This was to be a news item and time was marching on. The director was annoyed. At the end of the third week, however, the director startled me by throwing her arms around me to give me a hug. "Boy, am I glad you didn't write that press release!" A scandal involving the new teacher had forced the director to fire him. She was very happy the greater community would never know he had been involved with the school.

At the beginning of the next school year, a similar scenario took place. This time when the director asked me to write a press release, I immediately interviewed the three new teachers and, to the relief of the director, wrote the story right away. Then day after day I kept asking myself if I wanted to send the article out to the media. My answer was always no. By this time the director trusted enough in my Heartaculture to relax and be as curious as I was to find out why I didn't want to send the article. It wasn't long before we had our answer. One of the new teachers, who was a newlywed, decided the job was too much for her and resigned. A new teacher was quickly hired, and I just as quickly incorporated her into my story and sent it off to the media.

> *"Slow down and enjoy life. It's not only the scenery you miss by going too fast—you miss the sense of where you are going and why."*
>
> *Eddie Cantor*

In stressful situations I find that tuning in to my deeper sense of timing can offer relief. An example is when I am racing out the door to get to an appointment or to catch a plane because the clock says I am late. No matter how much time I allow myself to get ready, it seems I am always behind what I had planned. Over the years I have learned that instead of panicking when I rationalize that by clock time I won't get to where I need to be by the time I "need" to be there, I can simply attune to my body.

Even when my mind reasons I can't possibly get to the airport by the time my plane is scheduled to depart, I know I am doing fine if I am not feeling any inner tension. True, I may feel some physical tightness but my deeper self feels open and at rest. When I feel an inner calm all the way to the airport, I know the plane is going to leave late. This method has never failed me. It has, however, caused heart failure for other less-trusting people riding along with me!

I once had a visitor who needed to catch a train from a station that was eighty miles away from where I lived. As we leisurely ate our breakfast and she was packing up, I kept feeling at peace and knew we would make the train even though the clock said we should have already been on our way. I kept gauging our activities by the tension or lack of it in my body as we made choices about breakfast, took one more picture of each other, and exchanged last minute gifts. My friend never considered that we were leaving later than we "should" because I hadn't indicated to her that we needed to hurry.

It was only when we were about halfway to our destination that she noticed a highway sign that told her how far we still needed to go. She checked her watch and panicked. I remained calm and assured her we would have plenty of time. I told her I was certain the train would be late. She knew me well enough to know I was probably right, and agreed that she felt fine until she saw the sign and allowed her reasoning to make her anxious. Then she couldn't relax. She kept thinking about what she would do if she missed the train. Her "monkey mind" caused her stress.

When we arrived at the station about the time the train was scheduled to depart, there was no train in sight. Leaving me in the car, my friend jumped out and ran into the station. She soon returned all smiles. The train would be at least two hours late. We even had time for lunch!

Learning to trust heart-time allows you to respond to life more fully in present time. As you discover the code of internal motivation, and experience how it puts you in the right place at the right time for your best good regardless of deadlines or clock time, you will find yourself increasingly relaxed. When you relax, life can be more fun! You can take time to consider a wider range of options. This leads to increased creativity and a more fulfilling lifestyle. In turn it reinforces the hope that indeed maybe you CAN have what you want at your own pacing.

> *"There is more to life than increasing its speed."*
> Gandhi

Insisting on sticking to your rational plans and being "on time" no matter what is a good way to be continuously stressed. Also, it is very likely you will develop tunnel vision that doesn't permit spontaneity. Without spontaneity you cannot take full advantage of the universe's synchronicities as you can when you allow yourself to stay attuned to moment-to-moment changes through your present desires. Taking action as your heart wills it keeps you receptive to all the present moment's conditions and options. **When you stay "on call" to your internal signals, which indicate what your heart is wanting, you respond to the world with a more authentic you.**

Exercise 1

How to rely on heart-time

1. On a day when you have several errands to do, make a list of the tasks in the order you think you want to do them.

Example

       a) Pick up prescription

       b) Make bank deposit

       c) Get the car washed

       d) Do the grocery shopping

       e) Drop off film to be developed

2. When you are ready to start, consider the first task that you have listed. Ask, "Do I want to do this now?" Verify your response with your internal indicators.

3. If you do want to proceed, go ahead with the errand until it is finished or until you feel you want to do something different. If you do not wish to do the first errand, ask, "What would I rather do now?" Give yourself permission to do whatever it is you wish to do, whether it is the next errand on your list or something else. Proceed to do it until you are finished or until you want to do something different.

4. Consider the next item on your list. Repeat steps 3 and 4 until you complete your list or until you want to call it a day.

Remember to keep your "monkey mind" at bay by not giving credence to the "shoulds" or "shouldn'ts." For example, if you think, "I should get to the bank before 5 o'clock," rephrase to "I want to get to the bank before 5 o'clock." Then do not go to the bank until you really want to, no matter what time your watch shows.

How did your day go? Were your errands accomplished, or did you choose to do other things instead?

Were there some surprises or synchronicities? Were you happy about the outcome?

Learning to trust heart-time often means letting go of attachments to immediate results and seeing instead the benefits within the bigger picture. Perhaps when you didn't make a bank deposit when you thought you had to have it in, a customer calls later to request you hold his check, one that you were going to deposit, until he could put funds into his account the next day. If you had made the deposit as it appeared on your to-do list, it would have been returned to you by the bank with fees to pay.

Exercise 2

1. When you have a phone call to make, ask yourself, "Do I want to call now?" Verify your response with your internal indicators. Do not make the call until you feel a strong pull or inner impulse to do so. Avoid making the call only because you think you should.

2. When you do make the call, is the person you want to talk to available? Was the purpose for your call accomplished?

Chapter Seven

Aligning the Heart and Mind

Spiritual teachers throughout the ages have emphasized the power of the present moment. It is from the present that you create your future, whether that future is a minute from now or ten years away. Each day brings a new canvas of many present moments to create more of exactly what you want for tomorrow. When you ask yourself, "What do I want to do right now?" and open to the full gamut of options that the universe offers, in that instant you have tremendous power. In that brief interval of time, you have the opportunity to take one more step toward having more of what your heart wants—with full support of the

"The foolish man seeks happiness in the distance, the wise grows it under his feet."

James Oppenheim

universe. Each moment-to-moment choice you make based on internal motivation leads you closer to what your heart desires, even if you don't know exactly what that is.

Preventing Self-Sabotage

Living in the present moment means that your life express-es who you are now, not who you were ten years ago or even yesterday. When you make internally based choices, you con-stantly update your life to express who you are currently. On the other hand, externally motivated decisions based on what you think you want, or on goals you set for yourself in the past, may aim you in a dif-ferent direction than where your heart is pulling. You may still be focused on a path you chose for yourself five or twen-ty-five years ago that has little to do with the person you have become or what opportunities the universe offers today.

"We did not change as we grew older; we just became more clearly ourselves."
Lynn Hall

When the mind and heart are in conflict, what you truly want to create will be more difficult to manifest. Your focus and intent become muddy as the two parts of you rival each other, like competitive siblings, to create a sub-conscious self-sabotage. Instead of getting more of what you want, you may feel you are getting less or going nowhere.

You may feel bored or dissatisfied with your job, for example, and would love to do something else but don't know what that is. Or possibly you know what you want but are afraid to make a change for fear of losing the ben-efits, security, or prestige you currently receive. If you insist on staying in the job when you really don't want to be there, you may subconsciously make choices that eventually get you fired. You may become less productive, make mis-takes frequently, or take longer and longer lunch hours.

When the mind puts up obstacles to abiding by the heart's lead, the heart will do its utmost to bring about a change of mind, through the subconscious, in the most beneficial way. If the mind continues to stymie the course set by true desires—the underlying motivator in your heart of hearts—the stage is set for a rude awakening, an interrupter to the current path adhered to.

> *"Rowing harder doesn't help if the boat is headed in the wrong direction."*
>
> *Kenichi Ohmae*

This could be in the form of an unexpected layoff, an illness, an accident, or some other slap-in-the-face or sobering development that will cause you to have to make a change in a manner that may be neither comfortable nor smooth.

Choosing Your Ideal

The quickest and least obstructive path to creating what you truly want is to have your mind and heart agree. Then you have the blessing of full universal support on your side. One way to assure this alignment is to deliberately take stock of your current situation and run it by your internal indicators, your feelings. Here is an exercise that helps you do just that:

Divide a piece of paper into three vertical columns.

1) In the first column write down all that you like in your present situation.

2) In the second column list all that you don't like.

3) Now take a look at what you wrote in the first column, and ask yourself how you feel about the good aspects of your present situation. What three words describe the feeling? Write them down.

4) Do the same with the second column, and sum up the total experience of what in your present situation

you don't like. What three words describe how this part of your life feels? Write them down.

This simple reality check combines the knowing of both your head and your heart and helps discern what you wish to keep the same and what you would like to be different. As long as you have come this far, why not choose to have more of what you want.

5) Think about what your ideal would be. Write this down in the third column. Then consider how having this ideal would feel. Describe the feeling with three words and write them down.

6) Now put that feeling into your body, as if you already had your ideal. Fill yourself up with that feeling from your toes to your head. How does that feel?

7) Make the choice to create this feeling in your life now, the feeling that you are holding in your body of your ideal already manifested.

8) Once you make the choice, take a deep breath. As you exhale release all thoughts and feelings about your ideal.

9) Decide on a small step you will take toward having your ideal.

Determining how you want to feel instead of deciding on a specific form for your ideal bypasses the limits of logic and language to more fully express what both the mind and heart want. It is easier to know how you want to feel in your life than knowing the best possible form for that ideal to take. The mind and heart merge in the transfer of the thought into a feeling.

When you hold the feeling of your ideal in your body, you are actually manifesting what you want temporarily, for what is manifestation but making something physical. Past that moment, however, you do not have a form to sustain the feeling in your body or in your life. Holding the feeling in your body even for a moment gives a clear message to your subconscious, "This is what I want," and creates a template for the universe to draw to you what you desire in the best possible form to create that feeling in your life. **Making a choice to have your ideal activates the Law of Attraction, which magnetizes you and draws to you whatever you are focusing on.**

To take full advantage of the potential of the universe, it is best not to be attached to the form of your ideal. If you desire a life partner, for example, you may imagine someone tall and blond with certain attributes. It is good to think about these characteristics to help you clarify what you want, but then imagine how you would feel if you had someone with these characteristics in your life. The specific attributes do not matter as long as you have the end result: how you want to feel in your relationship with this per-

"Do not dwell in the past, do not dream of the future, concentrate the mind on the present moment."

Buddha

son. Focus on the essence of what you want without specifying the form it has to be in. Perhaps you want to feel supported, creative, and nurtured in the relationship. If you had that, what would that give you? Perhaps joy. Joy then would be the essence of what you want to feel in the relationship. Let the universe with its infinite possibilities bring you joy in the best possible form. It will do a much better job than you can, even in your wildest dreams!

Your job is to ally your mind and heart, to unite them on the same track, and then stay in the present with moment-to-moment choices that are internally

motivated. Although there is no guarantee that you will obtain your desire, the likelihood is greater when the mind supports the heart and all your inner resources are focused in the same direction. Each internally motivated choice you make draws on the heart's wisdom to bring you a step closer to achieving more of what you really desire, in the most effective manner.

Surviving the Detox Period

If most of your choices in the past have been externally motivated, much of your life situation may be constructed of consequences not aligned with the heart. Once you choose to live "from the heart," your present life situation will begin to change. Circumstances created from choices not aligned with your heart will begin to transform. Your current situation may completely unravel, making it seem as if your whole life is falling apart. Indeed it may well be. Current situations may no longer support the person you have become. They may no longer be the best form to give you the essence you desire.

"Change is not merely necessary to life, it is life."

Alvin Toffler

As your life begins to transmute, you may find yourself frightened or exhilarated, or both! You may be fearful of the changes, not knowing where they will lead, but at the same time feel freer and more hopeful. This is the "detox period." The situations in your life that no longer serve your highest good begin to dissolve but are not yet fully replaced by more favorable forms. You rejoice in expressing more of your true Self, but at the same time mourn what you have known.

It can be a very unsettling time. Situations, no matter how miserable they are, can feel more comfortable than going through a change. Known situations at least are familiar and give a sense of security, whereas change brings the unknown. You may experience a mixed bag of emotions during this period. Some days you may feel very up and excited. Other days you may feel unmotivated and sad, without knowing why. The old forms are hard to give up, even when they do not serve your best good to fulfill your potential or give you the most satisfying life experience. Perhaps the location of the job you left was convenient or you enjoyed the people there. There may have been a long-term relationship that dissolved because your personal paths are no longer compatible. Even as you find it difficult or painful to release these situations, you will feel empowered as your life force increases. Your spirit will respond to the hope of having more fully what you yearn for.

> *"The only courage that matters is the kind that gets you from one moment to the next."*
>
> *Mignon McLaughlin*

The detox period may last a week or perhaps months, depending on the extent of changes that are occurring. It is a time to nurture yourself, have downtimes, and not push to be productive. It is a time to be in the flow, to give into your whims, and to get plenty of rest.

The events of this period may seem counterproductive as your mind tries to make sense of the path your heart takes to reach your ideal. By doing only what you want in each moment, it may seem that you are heading in the opposite direction from what makes sense in order to gain what you desire. Your logic will insist that if you are not productive in your old idea of what productive means, you will not get where you want to go. Relax and take the "risk" of trusting your heart-mind. When you allow your heart to do the driving, the ride is a straight course that relies on unseen realities your mind cannot envision. The path will lead out of the form that no longer serves you to the most effective path within your circumstances. This will not feel familiar, safe, or comfortable if it is a new experience for you. It takes conscious effort to allow yourself to sit and enjoy the view when your "monkey mind" insists you do this or that to make what you want happen. As you persevere through the detox period, little by little you will feel the "sense" of where your heart is leading. The wisdom of the heart will be more apparent and easier to trust as your life course runs more smoothly and is more satisfying.

Exercise

How to go beyond your mind's obstacles to determine and act on your heart's desires

1. Imagine that you have won a lottery of several million dollars. List what you will change in your life, if anything.

> **Example**
>
> a) Buy a new car
>
> b) Quit my job and do my art
>
> c) Travel
>
> d) Donate to charity
>
> e) Upgrade my wardrobe

2. For every change you list, write a small step to take now toward having the change you want.

> **Example**
>
> a) List the features I want in a new car
>
> b) Set aside one evening a week to focus on my art
>
> c) List the trips I want to take this year

d) Take 10% out of my next paycheck and donate to charity

e) Go through my wardrobe and list the additional clothes and accessories I want to add

3. Take the small steps.

4. Determine the small steps that come next and take them.

5. Repeat step 4 until you have completed the change you want to make or until you decide you no longer want it.

One of the most common obstacles to considering the reality of having what we really want is thinking that we do not have the financial means to make it possible. By removing this limitation from our minds, we allow our hearts to speak. Taking small steps toward what is desired will help draw the support of the universe to manifest it.

Chapter Eight

Expanding Your Options

Living by Heartaculture puts life into a whole new perspective. The only limits are those you establish for yourself. You take full responsibility for creating your life experience. As long as you are a free agent, not a prisoner or a child under the restraint of others, your options are boundless. In any situation, you have a choice. It may not look as if you have a choice because you do not like the consequences of the choices you see, but you do have a choice.

"Our only limitations are those which we set up in our minds or permit others to establish for us."

Elizabeth Arden

Often all we see is an "either/or" situation that looks like two possibilities, either option #1 or option #2. We get so caught up in worrying about which option to pick, especially if neither are quite what we want, that we don't consider there may also be an option #3, and possibly options #4, #5 and #6. Perhaps you want a new car and don't have the cash to buy one. What are your options? Maybe at first glance you see option #1 as having to earn more money, and option #2 as getting a loan from your bank. What other options do you see?

Unlike our Western culture with its overemphasis on logic, Heartaculture assigns equal roles to the heart and mind. In Heartaculture, it may appear that the heart has the major role, but the truth is that without the mind you cannot determine your options. Without options to consider, the heart has no choice to make. In Heartaculture, the mind determines the options and the heart picks which options to act on. When the heart and mind are aligned toward the same goals, they are an awesome pair capable of most anything.

If the mind is to do its job exceptionally well, to go beyond the "either/or" syndrome and think out of the box, it must drop the conditioned judgments about which options are good/bad, right/wrong, possible/impossible. In the car example, what other options do you see? Perhaps #3—Get a loan from a friend or a relative. #4— Go to a different bank. What else? Keep going. #5—Find a car you like and ask if you can do a trade for work or for something else. #6—A combination of the above: get a small loan from your father, work for some overtime pay and do a trade for the rest. Keep going. #7—Buy a lottery ticket and hope to win. #8—Go to a government car auction. #9—Lease a car. What else? Keeping going until you empty your mind of all the options you can think of, and then push it to the absurd: #10—Rob a bank, #11—Steal a car, #12—Beg for money on a street corner. Getting silly about it will help you get out of the box of conventional thinking. You will be surprised at what you come up with. Don't edit any of it yet.

Okay, you have your list of options. Now it is the heart's job to pick the best one to act on. Get into your feelings. First review your list, and then quickly cross off the options you know right off the bat you have no desire to do. No other reason is acceptable. Don't cross off a possibility because you think it would be too hard, impossible, or immoral to do; or keep it on the list because you think it is what you should do. If you start pondering the merits of an option, you are in your head. With the remaining alternatives, go down the list again and feel which one or ones jump out at you. Which one(s) feels the best?

The one that feels best is the one to act on. If more than one option feels equally good, arbitrarily pick one of them. If none of the choices on the list feels good, it is not yet time to act. Wait awhile and when you are ready, look at your options again. Don't act until something feels right.

Next, take a small step toward the choice you made. As in the car example, if you decide to look for another bank, your next step may be to check for a list of local banks in the phone book. Or a step may be to ask a friend for a recommendation. Make the step small enough so that you will be sure to do it. Once you complete one step, take another. Keep going until you have reached your goal, or you no longer want to go in that direction. Perhaps as you move toward the option you picked, an entirely new possibility will present itself. Let's say that you ask a friend for a bank recommendation, and the friend tells you about his favorite bank but then also mentions that his friend is selling a car you might be interested in. When you consider calling the friend, it feels better than calling the

> *"At first our dreams seem impossible, then they seem improbable, but when we summon the will, they become inevitable."*
>
> *Christopher Reeve*

bank. You talk to the friend and find the car you want at a price you can manage.

By taking action you change your position with the situation. Your perspective changes. Options emerge that were not visible before you acted. Your heart knows this and can steer you in the most advantageous direction. When a choice doesn't make sense but feels right, you may need to head toward it, not to achieve the option itself, but to realize a new possibility.

Imagine yourself on a giant, larger-than-life chessboard. The pawns closest to you are so large they block your view of where all the other pawns are. You can only see the pawns and empty spaces nearest you. These empty spaces are your options for your next move. You pick the space that feels the best and move to it. From your new position you can see other empty spaces, options you couldn't see from your first position. Feeling out these new spaces, you pick your next move, and so on, space by space, till you reach your destination across the board. This is how to work with your options when you live by Heartaculture.

When you decide on a goal, you may also formulate a game plan to achieve it. However, to expand your options, be flexible. As you feel out the steps one by one, consider alternative options as you go. You many even end up with a different goal altogether. A goal is only something to aim for, a direction in which to go. Do not let it become a "should." It is all right to change your mind, and in many cases it is smart to do so. Successful business executives know this. When the world changes, your situation changes. Shifting market trends are analyzed in order to work out a business strategy. Periodically this strategy is updated to accommodate the current situation. Using Heartaculture offers a new strategy for life that is based on a person's internal response to various options, which takes into consideration how each option feels in general—a red or green light—as well as in comparison to other options.

Using Your Ideal as a Goal

In picking a goal, always start with your ideal. Make it what you really want. A common error is to start with what you think is possible and limit yourself right off the bat. Choose to have what you really want, your ideal, and take a small step toward it. Remember not to get stuck on a specific form, i.e., what you think the end result should look like. It is the essence you want. The path will open as you feel your way along, choosing from the options that will appear before you.

> *"The only way to discover the limits of the possible is to go beyond them into the impossible."*
>
> *Arthur C. Clarke*

When you pick a goal that seems impossible to attain, it takes faith to move toward achieving it. Take the first step and keep picking up your foot for the next step. You may not know where you will put your foot next, but by the time you are ready to put it down, the ground will be there. Trusting grows easier with experience.

Imagine a landscape with a tall mountain in the distance. Your goal is to get to the other side of the mountain. From where you are standing you cannot see any possible way to achieve your goal. Step by step you move closer and still have no idea of how you will get to the other side. It is only when you stand at the base of the mountain that you see the tunnel that goes all the way through.

When my son was nine years old, and we were renting a small house that was part of a ranch, we decided we were ready for something different. Separately we each made a list of what our desires were. Our combined list included a house with two wings, so we could each have a bedroom with privacy and our own bathroom; plenty of storage space; an extra bedroom for guests that could double as an office; a family room; a greenhouse; wood-burning furnace; and a big yard with a stream or pond nearby. My son said he would love it if he could ride his bike to school instead of having to take the bus. I said I would love to have a hot tub. After our discussion, I said, "Let's go get it!"

We piled into the car and drove toward town, which was fifteen miles away. Our agreement was that as I drove if either of us had a whim to turn down a side road we would do so. Almost immediately my son yelled, "Mom, turn here!" We did and shortly came to a house with a "for sale" sign in front of it. We knocked on the door but soon realized the house was empty. We walked around and peeked into all the windows and toured the big yard and outbuildings. Liking what we saw, but noting that it wasn't our ideal, I wrote down the realtor's name. It was a starting place. As I drove into town to find the realtor, I wondered how in the world I could afford to buy a house! I had always rented before. This was a new option to consider.

The realtor was willing to explore creative ways to provide us with exactly what we wanted, even with our limited financial resources. To my surprise she suggested we build our ideal house. She found a business that sold house kits and offered financing for the land until the house was completed. Then because of the equity created, a bank mortgage could be acquired. This felt like a good direction to go in. I picked one of the house models the company offered and varied the floor plan to suit my son's and my ideal. We then found a lot that suited us, although it was still six miles from my son's school.

As I progressed, each step felt good—until I "tried on" the work and time involved in the building process. It felt overwhelming. Could I do this all myself? I visited other people who had already built their houses using these kits. They were all very pleased with the results and said the work was worth it. I was encouraged and continued going forward. I made agreements with my friends to trade my services for their help. One friend committed to be my guide in the building process.

Drawing the outline of the house floor plan on the land revved my excitement, but when I imagined actually beginning construction something didn't jibe. It wasn't long before I found out what. The owners of the land backed out of the sale before the closing.

Before I could think of looking for a different lot, another option presented itself. There was a rental available with everything my son and I wanted except for a hot tub. Even though the rent was more than I thought I could afford, my experience with pursuing the house-building option had empowered me. I knew I could trust that the money would come. I could handle the rent. The house was at the end of a dead-end street, within walking distance to the center of town. It sat on two house lots at the base of an undeveloped hill and there was a stream that separated our front yard from a large city park. My son's school was on the other side of the hill, less than a five-minute walk away.

> *"Being open to allowing anything is the process of creating alternatives. This process can create alternatives that did not exist before you needed them."*
>
> *Ceanne DeRohan*

Not long after we moved in, a new friend of mine came to visit. He didn't know about our list of desires for our home. He noticed a burned place in the deck at the front of the house that the former tenant's barbecue had caused. I told him the spot would soon be repaired. "You know," he said, "that would be a great place to build a hot tub. Let me build it for you as a gift." And he did!

Exercise 1

How to expand your perspective and stimulate the possibility of new options

Changing your usual routines will help spur a change in perspective, stir your creativity and stimulate your ability to see different choices.

1. Eat your breakfast in a different place than you are used to: outdoors, in the bedroom, sitting on the floor, or at a restaurant you have never been to before.

2. Sit or stand in a place where you normally wouldn't to carry out activities in your home. For example, sit on the floor while talking to family members, stand on a chair or a table while you talk on the phone, or sit in a closet to read a book or to meditate.

Other than feeling a bit strange, how does changing your usual routines affect you? Do you see things you haven't before? Doing things out of the ordinary can be energizing and stimulate creativity. If you are an employer, have your employees do something out of the usual before a brainstorming session to increase their productivity.

"The universe will reward you for taking risks on its behalf."

Shakti Gawain

Exercise 2

1. Pick one activity you did today and list three to ten options for how you could have done it differently.

Example

Activity: Writing a letter on the computer

Options:

a) Write it by hand

b) Use colored ink

c) Use several colors of ink

d) Use all capital letters

e) Use all lowercase

f) Write with pencil

g) Use words cut out of magazines

i) Write in a circle around the paper

j) Use colored paper

k) Use a note card

2. Next time you do this activity, use one of your listed options.

Keep your creative edge and enliven your life force by altering your routines often.

Chapter Nine

Disempowering Your Fear

Fear is a part of life. We are all afraid of something. Some fears are instinctual and help preserve our well-being, such as the fear of jumping from great heights. Then there are conditioned or learned fears: fear of being a failure, of being poor, of upsetting the status quo, of being different, of looking selfish, of being punished, of being criticized, of being wrong. These fears are often the reason we do things we don't want to do, or become frozen in destructive or limiting situations, or are deterred from attaining our desired goals. They keep us adhering to expected behaviors and proven or approved-of choices and inhibit our trying new things and taking risks.

"Courage is resistance to fear, mastery of fear— not absence of fear."

Mark Twain

You cannot help having these fears, but you can do something about them. You do not need to allow them to be the power in your life. When you start to trust feelings rather than logic to make your decisions, there is no track record on which to rely. It is an unfamiliar way of negotiating the world, and until proven by experience, it is a risk that can stir up apprehension. You want to believe that the universe will provide everything you need when you follow your inner promptings, but all the "what-ifs" and anxieties about possible negative consequences if the universe doesn't come through surface to cloud true feelings and evoke doubts. Family and associates often project their own fears by voicing concerns and conventional advice that mirror and magnify your uncertainties.

"What do you mean, you want to quit your job? You have a good job, and good jobs are hard to come by. If for no other reason, you should stay there for the benefits. You've worked hard to earn those benefits."

Relying on False Security

Even when following the conventional path of tried and true rationale, there are no guarantees. The difference is that the familiar path offers a sense of security. The fact that others have followed the same way with some success gives us comfort and a confidence that the path has validity. The security, however, is false. The fact that one person has adhered to a course of action and achieved certain results

"Our greatest enemies, the ones we must fight most often, are within."

Thomas Paine

does not mean that everyone following a similar route will experience the same outcome. The world is always changing, and everyone is different and has varying resources and abilities. One day you can make a substantial income as an independent farmer. The next day that may still be true, but not as likely. The fact that one person does it only means that it is possible. When a person has gone before us and succeeded in something we would like to do, we are encouraged but not guaranteed the same outcome. Even when we are successful, the security we think we have developed can be erased in an instant. These days the long-esteemed standard for optimal success and security—having a college education and a high paying corporate job—is no guarantee of continued security. Thousands of long-time employed executives are laid off daily, often with little or no advance notice.

Taking the Next Step

Trust in the universe comes with experience, and experience comes with taking a risk. There is no way around it that I know of. Taking risks generates fear. Most of these fears are about change and losing our sense of security. We want to be guaranteed that we will always have "enough" and will be comfortable. It takes courage to initiate change in order to pursue your ideals when the new situation is uncertain or unknown. Quitting a job

"I know that God will not give me anything I can't handle. I just wish that he didn't trust me so much."
Mother Teresa

without the certainty of a new job, even when the current position is unbearable, may put you at risk of losing relied-on income and benefits, intimate relationships, or the roof overhead.

The question is: Do you want to stay where you are, or is there somewhere further or different you want to go? Do you want your life to be more satisfying and fulfilling? Being clear that you want something different helps motivate you to accomplish it, in spite of the fear. When you know that you do not want to stay "badly enough" where you are, it is easier to bypass the fear and take a leap into the unknown. A more effective motivator, however, is to focus on what you want to create rather than on what you want to avoid.

An exercise mentioned in a previous chapter suggests putting the feeling of your ideal into your body as if you already had what you want. I find when I do this, the "taste" of what I want is so strongly infused into my being that I will do whatever it takes to manifest it.

Even with all the experience I have living Heartaculture, over twenty-five years, I still have my fear. It is especially strong when I have no clue as to how I will get from point "A" to point "D." I did this when I cut my ties to the past and moved from Massachusetts to Arizona. I felt what my life in Arizona could be and was willing to let go of my career, my marriage, and the security of my network of friends to take the leap. Each mountain I saw in the distance had a tunnel going through it when I arrived at the base. I learned not to fret about the mountains. Instead, I focused on the present and where my foot would be placed next. No, it was not easy (because of my fear). Yes, it was well worth it!

"You will either step forward into growth or you will step back into safety."

Abraham Maslow

There were times when I was terrified, when I let my monkey mind take hold and plunge me into my worst fears. Each time I pulled myself out of the abyss of my terror by asking, "What do you want?" I refocused myself by dangling the feeling of having what I want in front of me. It was this carrot that urged me forward and down-graded the fear. I knew that I did not want to remain where I was in my life. I knew this from sensing how my current life would feel in the future and experiencing the limitedness of it. I chose to have what I really wanted and not settle for less, to always keep moving toward my ideal.

Even if I never attained it, I would have far more than if I stood still.

Conquering the "What-Ifs"

Looking too far ahead and wondering how you will ever get to where you want to go is what creates anxiety in most of us. The most common worry is about money. Will there be enough up the road for necessities and emergencies? This is where insurance companies capture us. They are masters in selling to our fears. Their promise is that they will provide for us if and when certain circumstances occur, even if the odds of those circumstances ever occurring are quite high. They sell to our desire for a sense of security, which wavers when we let our monkey minds play with all the "what-ifs." If you can't think of all the what-ifs, the insurance companies will provide some for you! They will sell you dozens of kinds of insurance: health, life, malpractice, home, death, car, trip, credit card, warranty, shipping, pet, on the basis of the what-ifs. What if you get cancer today? What if you lose your way of making a livelihood, or your home burns down, or you get sued? What if your packages get lost? Granted, many of these things do happen, but next time you decide to buy optional insurance, notice whether you are buying because of your fears or because it feels best?

"With God in charge, I believe everything will work out for the best in the end. So what is there to worry about?"

Henry Ford

The fear of a lack of money is a hard one to squelch. Most people see money as the way to get everything they want. In other words, money is the power in their lives. The universe is filled with infinite vehicles for acquiring what you desire. Money is only one way. By insisting that money is the only answer, you cut short the possibilities that could make getting what you want easier, faster and more direct.

One of my clients chose to leap into the void and take a chance on Heartaculture. She quit her long-standing job as an elementary school teacher without knowing how she would support herself. All she knew was that she wanted a change. Her ideal was to live in the country and not have to work for a while. She wanted some time out and to live closer to nature while she determined her life course. She had a little money in reserve, but not enough to pay rent and support herself for very long. Instead of focusing on how she would get enough money to have what she wanted, I suggested she choose to have her ideal and then take a step toward it. The step she took was to tell everyone she knew that she was looking for a house in the country in which to live. Within a very short time she was offered an indefinite housesitting job. For four years she lived in a beautiful old country house, all utilities paid. In exchange she was asked to do a little interior painting and take care of the house and yard.

The universe responds to our needs and desires when we, consciously or subconsciously, send out a "call." As stated previously, being clear about what you want and consciously choosing to have it helps align all parts of yourself to create a distinct signal for "pulling in" what you want to manifest. When you focus on obtaining the money for what you want instead of the end result, you limit yourself. Earning money for what you want may be a step, but it could also become a detour. It may be what you think you have to do, not what you really want to do.

Keep focused on envisioning the end result and let the universe bring it to you in the best possible form via the wisdom of your heart. Acknowledge your fear, but don't act from it. List all the possible actions for a next step and choose the one that feels the best, in spite of your fear. A great way to earn money may come your way, but asking for a loan from a friend may feel better, even though you worry about how you'll pay it back.

Remain open and trusting as you take each small step. The results may surprise you as you allow the synergy of the universe to operate. Who knows? Perhaps after you ask a friend for a loan, she will give you the money as a gift. It may be the opportunity she was wishing for to repay you for your helpfulness to her in the past. Be careful not to jump at the first possibility to fulfill your need or desire just because it presents itself. Hold out for the "perfect fit," the option that your internal indicators respond to with an "aha!"

Imagining the Worst-Case Scenario

When the fear of lack of money, or any other fear, freezes you into non-action or causes extreme anxiety, facing the fear head on is an effective way to disempower it. You may be doing all you can to accumulate the money you think you might need, but there is also a nagging thought, "Will this be enough?" Instead of allowing that thought to persist and grow and sap your energy, stop and define your fear.

> *"As we are liberated from our own fear, our presence automatically liberates others."*
>
> *Nelson Mandela*

What is the absolute worst thing that can happen if you don't have enough money? Take this worst-case scenario and try it on as if it is happening to you. Close your eyes and imagine yourself in this situation. How does it feel? Then ask, "What is next?" See and feel what happens.

When I projected myself into this situation, imagining myself not having any money at all, it felt terrible. A knot formed in my stomach and I felt ready to die. When I asked, "What next?" I could feel aid coming to me—people I know, friends and family—offering me what I needed. It is not a situation I would choose, but if it were to happen, I know that I would survive and make it through. Experiencing the worse case scenario in this way defuses the fear of the unknown. It grounds the fear in a reality so it can be dealt with and released.

A client who was having difficulty in her marriage was terrified that her husband would leave her. The thought brought up all her insecurities about abandonment. Deciding she would confront her fear fully, she closed her eyes, took a couple of deep breaths to help herself relax, and then imagined that her husband had left her. She asked herself, "What next?" and waited with an open mind to see what would come. To her surprise, instead of feeling devastated, she felt a great relief! She felt much lighter and full of energy. The experience empowered her. From then on she had the courage to be more honest with her husband instead of fearing the consequences of telling him the truth.

Often we live life trying to avoid change or trying to sidestep unpleasant experiences, seeking instead to create a sense of security. Yet life is always changing and nothing is really secure. What we read in the newspaper, watch on TV or listen to on the radio gives testimony to this. Anything can change in an instant. Even in our own beds we are not secure. I received a harsh reminder of this when I heard on the news about a woman in the Midwest who was killed in the middle of the night when a high wind caused a tree to fall through the roof and crush her as she slept. It is not a pleasant thought that life could be snuffed out so quickly without warning, but it is certainly a reality that gets you to thinking: Are all the measures we take for "security," to avoid all the what-ifs, worth it?

Developing Inner Peace

Remember, focus is power. If you put your attention on what you fear, it is likely that you will create exactly what you are afraid of. Likewise, if you focus on putting one foot in front of the other as you move toward your chosen result, you are apt to succeed in manifesting it for yourself.

There is a difference, if sometimes subtle, between taking measures to be safe and acting from a fear of loss. You may lock the doors and windows of your house or car to keep them safe, or you can obsess about preventing the loss of what you have, purchasing complicated security systems and stocking up with weapons. Feel the difference in the energy of these actions. Neither will guarantee that your house or car won't be harmed. The obsession, however, is a strong energy that is likely to act as a magnet for drawing to you the very loss that you fear. It is the same universal force, the Law of Attraction, which brings to you from the universe that which you choose from the deepest part of yourself and put your energy into achieving.

"There is no security on this earth; there is only opportunity."

Douglas MacArthur

In our ever-shifting and transforming world, where change is the only certain thing, the best way to develop inner peace and keep fear to a minimum is to let go of dependence on outer circumstances for your sense of security. **The real security must come from within.** Ask yourself, what are the conditions that make you feel most secure? For most of us, our sense of security is based on our ability to handle whatever life brings. When you learn to trust your innate internal compass to always point you in the best direction for your overall good, you will find that your confidence for navigating through life's ups, downs, and uncertainties will increase. The unknown will evoke hope and possibility instead of fear. Exterior forces will not have the impact they once did. Instead of reacting with anxiety to life's circumstances, you learn to respond from a deeper place, a place of knowing and of conscious choosing.

When a door slams shut to obstruct the path you are on, you learn that another door will open, although it may take some time and patience on your part. The new opening is always better, though it may not seem better at the time, especially if you had expectations of a certain outcome. Down the road you will realize in retrospect that the altered path produced a more suitable outcome for you. You may even begin to be thankful for those times of setback if you learn to ask, "What is the opportunity here?" When what you were depending on doesn't happen or when the worst-case scenario becomes a reality, watch for the blessing.

As you build your repertoire of trust experiences, you will learn to rely on them when the universe doesn't seem to be working for you the way you think it ought to. Although fear will always be around to some degree, it will take a backseat when you allow your desires do the driving.

**What role do your fears play?
Are they a deterrent or an excuse?**

Exercise

1. Name a goal you want to reach but have not yet taken action to attain, such as move to the country in a year, ask my boss for a raise, take a lead role in a play, volunteer to be a Boy Scout leader.

2. List the reasons you have not yet taken action for attaining this desire. Are any of these reasons grounded in fear? Name the fear.

Example:

Goal: Learn to ride a horse

<u>Reason for not taking action</u>	<u>Fear</u>
a) I don't have a horse.	It will be expensive to rent a horse.
b) I am too old to learn.	I will make a fool of myself.
	I am not fit enough physically.
c) I don't want to ride alone.	I will fall off and not have help.

3. Ask yourself, "If all my fears were eliminated, would I want to have this goal now?" In the above example, if the expense wasn't an issue, the expertise came easily, and there was a friend to ride with, would you want to learn to ride a horse?

a) If the answer is yes, your fears are acting as a deterrent from going for your goal. Prevent them from having further power over you by taking a small step now toward attaining your goal. Make the step small enough to be sure you will do it. Once you take the step, take the next one and so on until you have achieved your goal or you decide it is no longer what you want. In the horse-riding example, a step may be to call the local stable to find out how much lessons cost. Another step could be to ask a friend to take lessons with you, or to start doing stretching exercises. By taking steps one by one in spite of your fears, you empower yourself for creating more and more of what you want in your life.

b) If the answer is no, this goal is most likely not one you really want, or at least not one you want now. More likely it is something that you thought you should want, or that you decided sometime in the past you wanted but you no longer care to have. Your supposed fear is an excuse for not taking action toward something you don't want now. If you feel that the goal is something you do want, decide on a date when you will reconsider taking action toward your goal.

Chapter Ten

The Consequences of Compromise

Late in his life my father confessed to me that he had always wanted to be an English teacher. Instead of following this desire, he gave in to his father's wishes and become a certified public accountant. The reasoning was that CPAs make more money than teachers, which would allow my father more "success." As anticipated, my father made a good living as an accountant and was a capable provider for our family. After work, however, my father was often tired and grumpy. It was only when he was fully relaxed, usually on family outings, that I saw him come alive. On vacations he was so different from how he usually was in our daily life, telling jokes and leading

> *"Getting fired is nature's way of telling you that you had the wrong job in the first place."*
> Hal Lancaster

family songs, that I called him "Uncle" instead of "Dad." When my father acknowledged that he hadn't followed his heart's desire, he reflected on how different life might have been had he become the teacher he wanted to be.

Compromise is giving up on achieving or obtaining what you really want. It is not going after your dreams, or what really matters to you, or stopping before you achieve them. To please his father, my father didn't pursue his desire to be an English teacher. He had a good life and seemed happy enough, but I wonder how much more spirited and fulfilling his life could have been had he been more passionate about his occupation. He worked eight hours a day for over forty years, a good proportion of his life, focused on something less than what he really wanted. I think he had satisfaction in his work and even moments of passion, but was it the best choice for expressing his inner self or for experiencing the deepest fulfillment? He could have pursued his love for English or for teaching in other ways, but most of his time and energy was devoted to making a living and maintaining a household and family. I don't think he regretted his choices, but I believe he could have had more of what he wanted and been more fulfilled had he been open to alternative options.

"Many of life's failures are people who did not realize how close they were to success when they gave up."

Thomas Edison

Life is filled with choices and perhaps we can't have it all. There isn't enough time and energy to pursue all our desires, but when we make choices that close the door to obtaining what matters to us, that is compromise. Many of our daily, transitory, "surface" desires that go unsatisfied are soon forgotten. It is the deeper desires that I am talking about, the ones that are perhaps covered over by present priorities but are still there. They don't go away.

The Power of Hope

There are many reasons for not pursuing what matters to us, the most common one being the belief that what we want is impossible to have. We do not see our options. If your salary barely covers your necessities, you may believe taking your dream vacation to Hawaii is impossible. If you are a single mother of four children, you may not see a way to go back to school and get a degree. Other reasons for not pursuing our heart's desires include not wanting to displease people who are important to us, as in the example of my father, or giving into one or more of our fears.

> *"The mass of men lead lives of quiet desperation. What is called resignation is confirmed desperation."*
>
> *Henry David Thoreau*

Whether you recognize it or not, whenever you compromise by making choices that do not take you toward what is important to you in any area of your life—your work, relationships, personal growth or environment—you are choosing not to realize your full potential. Each time you give up something that matters to you, a part of your life force closes down. You accept that you will never have what you hope for. You become hopeless about that aspect of your life.

Feel for a moment what "hopeful" feels like. Imagine applying for the high-paying job that you want. Your interview goes well and you know that you have a good chance of being hired. What does this feel like? Most likely it feels good. Perhaps it enforces a sense of direction and purpose for your life or stirs up thoughts about what you could do with the higher income. The hope of new possibilities creates an open-endedness in your life—something good can happen. Even if the result is that you don't get the job, at least you took a step toward what you wanted and you know the possibility is there.

Now imagine the opposite. What does "hopeless" feel like? Imagine that when you go to apply for the job, you discover that dozens of better-qualified applicants have already been interviewed. Instead of applying you decide this was your last chance to get the job you always wanted. You leave and go back to the unfulfilling position you've held for thirty years. How does it feel when you imagine accepting that you won't ever get what matters to you, so you see yourself giving up? Feel the difference in your body when you try on each of these scenarios.

Each time you become hopeless about some aspect of your life, you disconnect from a piece of your heart. A part of you closes down, suppressing your inner expression and sacrificing a part of your being. You are "disheartened." You may feel this as a contracting or shutting down.

When the streams feeding a river dry up or are blocked, the flow of the water in the river is affected. The river no longer fills its whole bed, its full capacity. It is not the river it once was or that it could be. Likewise, our life force is fed by the motivations created by our true desires, the deeper longings of our hearts. If these mainsprings for life are diminished by losing hope that our desires will be fulfilled, our life force also diminishes. When we no longer give credence to our dreams and hopes, we lose the incentives to live life to its full capacity. Our energy and creativity wanes. We give in to living solely for survival or to maintaining the status quo.

On the other hand, knowing we can pursue our desires if and when we are ready keeps the channels fully open for our life force to flow. Where there is hope there is potential. The difference between totally abandoning our desires and choosing to take action in the future is the difference between a closed or open door to self-expression.

Obvious examples of despair caused by hopelessness are easy to spot among the homeless and poverty-stricken, but similar hopelessness in our own lives can be harder to discern. When we live comfortably—a nice house, plenty of food on the table, and ample savings account—we may not think to define our frequent illnesses, workaholism, chronic TV watching, or consistent tiredness as symptoms of hopelessness. However, these indicators can result from relinquishing our heart's desires to maintain customary actions or standards that we think are necessary or expected of us. Until a disruption in routine or dramatic crisis rocks the boat and jolts us back to hearing our hearts, it is often simpler to row along merrily, or not so merrily, without consulting or paying attention to our inner compass.

> *"Perhaps the most important health warning of all is to 'have a heart'."*
>
> Dr. Paul Pearsall

The Toll of On-Going Compromise

Heartaculture is about corroborating with the heart at all times, not only when it is convenient or easy. If you compromise with the smaller choices on a daily basis, compromise gradually becomes a habit: going to a party to please your spouse instead of staying home and reading a book; painting the kitchen green instead of the blue you prefer because you already have green paint on hand; agreeing to babysit your grandchild when you would rather work in the garden. These are the types of easy compromises that we can make on a daily basis. They seem like very small sacrifices, but on an ongoing basis, they can erode your quality of life by diminishing your relationship to yourself and to others. When you give up something that matters to you, you negate yourself. You go against your deeper knowing of what will take you toward deeper personal fulfillment.

If you have a strong desire to go to the beach, but then you let a friend talk you out of it and you go to the ballgame instead, does it really make a difference? Use your internal indicators to know when you are compromising. If you have a strong body response to an option, pay attention. When you decide to go to the ballgame instead of to the beach, is there a tension within you? Is it momentary or does it sustain? If it releases when you put your full focus on the game, then being at the beach at that moment is not all that important to you, and you are not compromising by going to the game. If, however, you decide to go to the game and the tension in your body remains, pay attention. Your desire to go to the beach is motivated from a deeper part of yourself and indicates that for some reason your yearning needs to be satisfied. It could be that you need the sun and soothing quality of the water, or perhaps there is someone there you need to meet or who needs to meet you. There could even be danger associated with going to the game. Whatever the reason, when you compromise, you take away from your life, whether it is a temporary effect or a life-changing consequence.

Even when the obvious effect of one compromise seems small and momentary, the result of multiple compromises over a period of time can lead to a general dissatisfaction or frustration in life and eventually to depression or illness. A sure clue that someone is compromising, either temporarily or constantly, can be evidenced by a negative disposition. The next time a person in your life (including yourself) is irritable, angry, rebellious, withdrawn, listless or hostile, ask him or her, "What are you doing that you don't want to do?" If his or her normal modus operandi is compromise, the answer may well be a grumpy, "Everything!" Then ask, "What would you rather be doing?" When the reply is a vague, "I don't know," you may need to dig a bit to uncover habitually suppressed or pent-up desires.

Doing things you really do not want to do can be as great a compromise as not doing what matters to you. Again, pay attention to your body indicators. Is the action momentarily displeasing to you, or do you have a stronger, deeper negative response to it?

Choosing to Have What Matters

Take time now to review your persistent desires and aversions. What have you pushed aside in favor of more pressing priorities? List what you have always wanted to do but haven't yet done. Look at these desires now in the light of Heartaculture. Whatever the reason for not pursuing what you have always wanted, give yourself permission to do so now.

Make a plan for each of your wishes. Choose to take a small step toward obtaining them, or pick a date in the future when you will reassess them again. If you choose not to go immediately toward what matters to you, it is important that you decide to pursue it whenever you are ready. Choosing a specific time up the road for reevaluation enlivens the possibility of having what you want, and thus energizes your life force. Feel the

"The greatest mistake you can make in life is to be continually fearing you will make one."

Ellen Hubbard

differences between giving up what you want, deciding to pursue it someday, and taking a step toward it now. What feels best?

For the things you are doing that you do not want to do, ask why are you doing them. List the main reason for each one. You may not like the immediate consequences of a different choice, or you may like the results the current actions bring. Whatever the reasons for doing what you do not want to do, give yourself permission not to do it. What happens when you decide not to do it? How does it feel? You may discover that on a deeper level you are doing what you want to do. Know that you do have a choice! It may not look like you do, but you do. If you don't like the alternative choices you see, can you expand your options?

For many situations, compromising what matters to you can be avoided by releasing your idea of what form is needed to satisfy your desire. Open up to other options when what you want seems difficult or impossible to have. Name as best you can the essences you think you will get by having what you want: What are the qualities, feelings, or crucial elements you hope for?

Using the beach example, what is the essence that going to the beach would give to you? Do you want to relax and be nurtured? Are you craving the warmth of the sun or a change from your usual routine? If you had exactly what you wanted, what would it feel like? Perhaps sensual, peaceful, and restful are the qualities you hope for. If going to the beach is not an option for one reason or another, what other choice could give you the same satisfaction—perhaps getting a massage or staying a night at a luxury hotel with a pool and spa? Imagine yourself having a massage and feel the experience as if it were happening now. Does it hold the qualities you are hoping for? Keep thinking of alternatives and trying them on until you find a form that can fulfill the essentials of your desire.

"Most people would rather be certain they're miserable, than risk being happy."

Robert Anthony

There is always a way to pursue the essence of what you want even if the form you hope for is not an option. If you are physically disabled, playing football on a major league team may not be an option. Competing and excelling on some other sort of team, whether in sports or business, is a possibility. You may not have what it takes to be a famous movie star, but what other options would give the attention, glamour, or satisfaction you crave? Whether it be a need or a desire, find a way to fulfill it in some form. For example, you can take a home study course to achieve your educational goals rather than attend college in person. Instead of building your dream home right now, couldn't you make changes to your present home that would give you more of the qualities you desire?

Instead of giving up on what you desire, knowing the door is open whenever you choose to walk through will make a big difference in how you feel. As you choose those options, both trivial and important, that take you toward what matters most to you, you allow your life force to flourish and give yourself the best chance of finding fulfillment.

How to stop compromising and have more of what you want in your life now

Exercise

1. Go back to the exercise for Chapter 7. If you had an extra several million dollars, how would you change your life? The changes that you list will most likely be in the areas of your life where you are compromising now.

2. For each change you want to make, list the final result you want. For example, if you want to buy a new car, describe the car you see yourself having. If you want to travel, describe the place you most want to travel to.

3. Shut your eyes. Take a deep breath and relax. Imagine yourself having or doing the end result you described. How does it feel? What are the qualities or essences you feel that are satisfying to you from this end result? Choose to have these qualities in your life now.

4. Open your eyes and write down the qualities or essences that you want from each of the changes you listed. How can you have more of these qualities in your life now while taking the small steps toward having the change you want? List alternatives for having the qualities you desire for each change you want to make.

Example

Change: Travel more

Essences: Adventure, change of pace, fun, stimulation

Alternatives: Eat at a new restaurant once a week

Go on short day trips to new places

Ask an acquaintance along to a local event

Register for tango lessons

5. Choose one or more alternatives to do each week. At the same time, continue to take the small steps toward having the change you want until your desire is satisfied. You may find that the alternative actions you take fulfill the essences you yearned for, so that the original change you thought you wanted is no longer a desire.

Chapter Eleven

Living Heartaculture with Others

By now you have an idea of how to live by Heartaculture. Hopefully you are experimenting with it and are experiencing the results of a more authentic lifestyle, one that expresses more of the real you. As you grow comfortable with the concepts of Heartaculture, you will wonder how to apply them when living with other people, both at home and in the workplace. If everyone is doing only what they want to do, won't there be continuous conflicts? Won't it be difficult to be productive? My experience has been the opposite.

> *"Your natural reluctance to unbalance the rest of the family stops each of you from changing."*
>
> *Lynne Bernfield*

The first person that agreed to live Heartaculture with me was a fairly new acquaintance. Soon after I relocated from Massachusetts to Arizona, she announced she was leaving New Hampshire to come and live in the same town where I was. We agreed that she and her nine-year-old daughter would stay at my home until she could get settled in her own home.

At that time my young son and I lived in a small two-bedroom mobile home. As my friend was navigating across the country on her way out West, it suddenly dawned on me how little I knew about her and how crowded our situation would be. As soon as she arrived I expressed my concerns and suggested that the only way I could imagine the situation working well for all of us was if we lived by Heartaculture. The sole ground rule we established was that both of us would do only what we wanted when we wanted. We would only cook, shop, clean, be with the children or with each other when we wanted. There was no obligation on my part to accommodate her needs and no obligation on her part to "pay me back" for her visit by doing things for me.

It was wonderful! I found I wanted to cook most of the meals, but had no desire to clean up afterwards. My friend said she had no desire to cook but enjoyed washing the dishes. The one time I didn't want to cook she came to me, before I mentioned anything, and said she wanted to cook dinner. We laughed when I told her I had no desire to cook that evening but felt like cleaning up. We did most everything together with both of our children, but one day I longed for solitude. Again, without knowing how I felt, my friend said she wanted to take the children hiking—Did I want to come too? Another day, it was the reverse: I wanted to take off with the kids and asked my friend if she wanted to come along. Then it was she who wanted to be alone. Our days flowed easily and harmoniously, but after a month I was ready to have my home to myself again. The very day I planned to talk to my friend about it, she announced she had found a house to rent and would move into it shortly. Again we laughed at the synchronicity that characterized our entire Heartaculture experiment.

Living True to Yourself in Harmony with Others

When people agree to live by Heartaculture, the results can be wondrous. There is a smoother flow of activity, and somehow the important things are accomplished easily. Not feeling controlled by our feelings of being obligated to other people is very liberating and fosters empowerment, creativity, and affection.

Most of the time, however, we are involved with people who are not consciously following their hearts. They may think they are doing what they want, but often their choices are defined by a conditioned reality that limits what is possible and allowable and what is not. It is a reality of constant compromise. Herein lies the challenge. How do you live Heartaculture when faced with the limited views and continual judgments of those around you? How can you be true to yourself and keep in harmony with the different wishes and needs of the group of individuals with whom you live or work? It is possible! This is where the art of Heartaculture comes in. It takes consciousness, practice, dedication and persistence to be good at it, but any new steps toward being more authentic will bring positive results on some level.

"Everyone is born with genius, but most people only keep it a few minutes."

Edgard Varese

You may feel empowered and at the same time feel uncomfortable about the temporary disharmony created between you and other people. Remember the "detox period." As you begin to act from your heart with others, it may take some time to undo those patterns set in motion from your "old" self. If, for example, you have agreed to an action that others are depending on and suddenly, you say, "Forget it, I just realized I don't want to do this!" you may create some resentment. It could be best for all concerned that you honor your agreement and compromise this time to keep harmony. Then vow to yourself that next time you will not take on anything that doesn't feel right. Realizing and admitting you do not want to carry out your agreement will "right" the "crooked energy" (as a friend calls it) within you and between you and others. Most likely it will be a subtle rather than an obvious shift, but the correction will empower you with yourself and in relationship to the group. You will feel more open.

When you are ready to live Heartaculture in a more expanded way, i.e., with others as well as when you are by yourself, there are some helpful basic steps. The first is to be committed to the outcome—each person being true to him or herself while attaining the shared goals of the group. This can work for a couple, a family, partners and associates at work, an organization, or any gathering of people. You want the greatest good equally for all involved. With this mindset, your heart-will is open to the universal level to bring the most favorable benefit possible to each person.

Second, stay attuned to your inner indicators by continuously asking, "Is this what I want to do right now?" This is a crucial step to keep you "honest" with yourself and others.

Third, if the proposed action does not feel right for you, modify it until it feels good. If your son wants you to drive him to his friend's house right now, is this what you want to do? If it feels fine, that's great. If it doesn't, feel how it would be to do it another time, perhaps in fifteen minutes, or tomorrow. Do you want to do it at all? If not, be honest with your son. Suggest other options for him to obtain what he wants. Perhaps someone else could drive him, or he could walk, ride his bike, take the bus, or get a cab. If you feel strongly about not wanting to drive him, and neither of you can think of an option that is suit-able for both of you, going to his friend's house at that time is not an option. But Dad . . . ! But Mom . . . !

> *"I have found the best way to give advice to your children is to find out what they want and then advise them to do it."*
>
> Harry S. Truman

This may seem a hard line, but try it and see what happens. You may think, "It is a little thing. I really could do it." The fact that you could do it is not the point. If you really don't want to do it, don't! When you do some-thing for someone else that you don't want to do, you will feel some resentment. Resentment erodes relation-ships, especially when it grows. And by not being true to yourself, you negate the possibility for the situation to change and evolve into something even better for every-one concerned.

An example of this is when a friend of mine realized that she didn't want to go camping on the weekend as had been planned with her husband and son. She was afraid to tell them for fear they would be hurt or angry, but she finally took the risk. They were disappointed but decided to go anyway. The result was that they enjoyed a rare father-son experience and my friend was rejuvenated by her time alone. She appreciated her husband and son all the more when they came home.

When you choose not to do something that someone requests, another possible outcome is that the person will realize they didn't really want to do whatever it was in the first place. They may have only felt an external pressure to do it. In the driving-the-son-to-his-friend's-house example, the son may be inwardly relieved that he has no way to get to where he says he wants to go. Now he has an acceptable excuse to tell his peers for something he really didn't want to do.

Co-Creating Mutual Fulfillment

If you are working with two or more people, and an idea or projected action doesn't feel right to you, speak up. Then ask the others what results they want or what essences are desired. Keep working at the form for the action until it includes the main qualities that are desired or until it feels good, or right, to all of you. By doing it this way, the result is a much better form than could be imagined at the start. I call this "co-creation." It is a process by which each person, by being true to his or herself, can contribute the "genius" of his or her being toward the fulfillment of the group goal.

For three years I worked a business where my two partners and I made our decisions this way. We were amazed at what shaped up when we persisted in tweaking the form to feel right to all three of us. The results were far beyond what any one of us could have created on our own, and the process became an enjoyable adventure as we anticipated the wondrous collective ideas we would generate.

When the group is big, this process can be just as exciting and productive, but if the time is limited, not all involved may feel fully satisfied. When the process is curtailed before the form feels right to everyone, it is important that dissatisfied individuals not abandon the essences they want. To remain true to themselves (and thus to the group) they can explore other options to fulfill the qualities they feel are lacking. Perhaps modifications to the group decision can be added later.

I have used this process in organizations to create mission statements and to solve problems that were difficult to solve any other way. It also works well in families. When everyone is included in the process of finding a way to achieve a common goal, the ownership of the solution is much stronger. The motivation for adherence is built in when the form contributes to everyone's satisfaction or sense of personal fulfillment.

> *"Treat people as if they were what they ought to be, and you help them to become what they are capable of being."*
>
> *Johann Wolfgang von Goethe*

It was my son's job to put the dishes in the dishwasher and clean up the kitchen after dinner. He consistently forgot and I had to remind him, which I did not want to do. I wanted him to want to do it as part of his contribution to the household. Dream on, right?

I made the decision not to remind him and, predictably, the kitchen did not get cleaned. For two nights I worked around the mess until there were no clean pans to cook with. On the third night my son came to me and asked, "What's for dinner?"

"I don't know," I answered. "Since all the dishes are dirty, I have nothing to cook with!" He got my point. I told him that when he doesn't do his part, I can't do mine. He had to put together his own dinner that night, experiencing the direct consequence of his actions, or non-action.

This opened the door for further discussion. I expressed my frustration and anger about having to continuously remind him to do what I asked him to do. In retort, he complained about having to do what I "made" him do. "You're right," I agreed. "We need to decide together what needs doing."

We began by discussing the kind of household we wanted, what standards we could agree to. Next we itemized the actions needed to maintain those standards. We made up a job chart for the routine chores and negotiated as to which of us would do what and when. We opted to have consequences for not doing our assigned tasks. Surprisingly my son concocted more drastic consequences than I ever would have. I helped modify them, and we also laughed about some silly ideas we had thought of.

The result of this co-creation was two much-happier people! The jobs got done with more of a teamwork spirit, and when the occasional consequence needed to be lived out, it wasn't such a big deal. It helped to have me "forget" my chores occasionally to keep the tally more even. I also allowed, whenever possible, for my son to discover his own omissions rather than me pointing them out. This helped remove me from the ogre position I despised and helped him develop self-responsibility.

Empowering Authentic Self-Expression

Co-creation takes open minds. It won't work well if people are attached to their ideas or ways of doing things. To help the co-creative spirit, trust must be established. People who feel valued know that their opinion counts and will be heard without them having to engage in power struggles to present their point of view.

Living by Heartaculture empowers authentic self-expression. It creates a culture of mutual respect and trust, thus fostering creativity and productivity. To establish this way of interaction in the relationships or groups in which you are a participant, use the same modes that you do with yourself:

1. Honor other people's desires without judging them.

2. Insist that everyone does only what they want to do. (Do not impose "shoulds" on anyone.)

3. Encourage trust and the expression of feelings.

4. Inspire hope and creativity by suggesting options for fulfilling desires.

5. Help waylay fears by emphasizing the power of choice and staying in the present moment.

Honor other people's desires without judging them.

Listen to wishes without labeling them as good, bad, right or wrong. Your judgments are part of your own conditioning or fears, not about the other person's desires. Remember, desires are expressions of the heart and therefore can tell you about the person, their current needs, or perhaps what they are perceiving intuitively.

"I wish I could be a circus clown."

"A clown? That's different. What appeals to you about being a clown?"

"I could make you laugh and then you would want to be with me more."

Insist that everyone does only what they want to do.

Doing *only* what you want to do is different than doing *anything* you want to do. It means that within the options you see for yourself, you don't do something unless you want to. This can be a hard one, especially if you are counting on people to cooperate and follow a plan you have devised, or if you have asked others to participate in an activity that you have your heart set on. (Children are a special case that will be discussed later.)

Heartaculture is about allowing the truth within us to surface and be expressed. If someone does not want to do what you want them to, you may have uncomfortable feelings to deal with. The truth is not always pleasant. The reality that your spouse does not want to accompany you to an office party may make you feel angry or unsupported. This is for you to look at, not to make your partner feel guilty or wrong for not having the same desire as you. Remember, he can't help how he feels. It may, however, say something about your relationship. If neither of you ever want to do the same things and it bothers you, perhaps it is time to talk about what is going on between you. You can reexamine your needs and desires, and discuss how both of you will get your needs met.

My experience with relationships is that when each person agrees to do only what he or she wants to do, much pressure is relieved. People are given space to be their own authority and take self-responsibility. They can be honest with themselves and with you. Resentments virtually disappear. Of course there may be a "detox" period if you are used to doing things only to please each other, but once you get used to living this way, it can be heaven.

During the detox time you may fight with your monkey mind, which is busy obsessing over reasons why the other person does not want to do either what you want to do or what you want them to do. You may feel hurt or abandoned if your partner says, "I want to be alone right now," imagining it has something to do with you. If you hold the conditioning that only full "togetherness" is a successful relationship, you will conclude that your relationship is failing when your partner does not want to do what you want to do. To weather the detox, the inner quibbles you may have, focus on the end results you want: a more positive and authentic relationship, greater intimacy, and inner-motivated teamwork.

Hopefully you will eventually get to the point of accepting that a desire can be just that, a desire, and not see it as having meaning beyond that. If the desire is coming from the heart and not externally motivated, there will be no rational reason, just the "I want" or "I don't want." It is not a reflection on or about you. By accepting this and not being critical of that desire, you honor the person's authentic self.

The best relationships I know are based on allowing loved ones to express exactly who they are. Difficulties arise when we insist on coercing people into doing things they really don't want to do to win our love or favor.

There is nothing wrong with encouraging a person toward an action you hope he or she will take because you think he or she will enjoy it or benefit by it, or because you want his or her company. Sometimes a nudge helps a person overcome a fear or an externally produced resistance: having too much to do, not having enough money, not wanting to go against the norm. What you don't want to do is bypass a person's heartfelt feelings.

Sometimes these can be hard to discern. Once you have given your nudge, give the person full permission to do what they think they want to do without further discussion. No nagging! After hearing your words and having space to live with their decision, and perhaps the consequences, the person may get to a deeper level of feeling and realize that what you suggest is what they want after all.

If you practice this approach consistently, you will develop a deeper trust and mutual respect in your relationships. Think about how you would like to be treated.

Observe in your current interactions with others how you feel when someone tries to convince, persuade, or coerce you to do as they wish you to, no matter what his/her motive. How do you feel toward him/her when he/she does this? How does it affect your relationship and sense of trust? If you feel pushed, does your guard go up? How does this affect your sense of intimacy with that person?

In a work, family, or organizational environment, a common concern about living in the Heartaculture mode is that nothing will get done or priorities won't get taken care of. People, in their heart of hearts, want to feel useful and effective. When you use the co-creative approach to determine how common goals are to be achieved, you will find that individuals want to do their part. The discipline for a manager, director, or parent is to allow others to do their part in the way they wish and at their own pacing, within the time and quality parameters that have been collectively established.

The time to pay attention is when people don't want to do what they've agreed to. Recall the example of my not wanting to get news releases written or sent out when my director was asking for them. Does your employee or child have a rational reason for not wanting to do the task, or do they just not want to do it? Perhaps the not-wanting-to-do is an intuitive insight that will become more obvious later. Decide together to give it more time or find an option that feels right to both parties.

Occasionally you will find an employee who never wants to do his or her job, is constantly feeling dissatisfied, or has a continually negative attitude. Perhaps this person is in the wrong environment or position for their greatest good. Ask: If they could do anything they wanted, what would they want to do? What are the essences they desire in their work? Does the current work situation fulfill those qualities, or is it time for a change? What are the options?

Encourage trust and the expression of feelings.

When asked what they want to do, most people will react quickly and tell you not what they really feel but what they think is "right" to do in the circumstances. You may have to work a bit to draw them out.

> "Tom, do you want to go to the store with me?"

> "Sure, I will go if you want me to."

> "Is there something you would rather do right now?"

> "Now that you ask, yes, I really want to finish this letter I'm writing."

If you consistently make it safe and not react when others tell you their true wishes, the truth will be more easily forthcoming. They won't feel they have to hold back and shield you from something you don't want to hear, or themselves from your possible negative reaction. If they feel that you accept them unconditionally, they will be able to go deeper within themselves and share much more with you.

At one point in a long-term relationship I was in with someone who was not comfortable in expressing his feelings, I asked that we relate to each through Heartaculture. My significant other was cautious at first but agreed. He admitted he was afraid he would hurt me if he always told me his true feelings. I challenged him to try me out. Soon after our agreement, I surprised him one day by dropping in at his home office without warning. He was not his usual welcoming self.

> "Is this not a good time for me to be here?" I encouraged.

"I'm in the middle of something," he said warily, with a look that told me he was testing me.

"Oh, I'm sorry, is there a better time for me to be here?" I responded.

"How about tomorrow?"

"That works for me. What time would be good?" I asked as I massaged his shoulders. He responded with a radiant smile and gave me a warm send-off when we parted.

By accepting his wishes without acting rejected, I signaled to him that he could express his feelings without suffering whiplash from me. Although I was disappointed that I couldn't spend time with him at the moment, I felt the reward of his deepening appreciation of me and the excitement of reaching a new place in our relationship. Our communications with each other became more open and frank, which contributed greatly to an increased intimacy and satisfaction.

Asking others to be truthful with you about their feelings will force you to be more honest with yourself. It starts a snowballing effect for the good. As the people in your life open up more to you with their authentic expression, you can express new levels of your feelings toward them in return.

Inspire hope and creativity by suggesting options for fulfilling desires.

Hope is crucial to the human psyche. We can withstand most anything if we feel the possibility of obtaining what we want. It is a great motivator and lifter of moods. As long as a carrot is dangling in front of us, we will take another step, hoping it will get us what we are aiming for or at least bring us closer. Encourage each person in your life to consistently take steps toward fulfilling his or her dreams (toward their carrots) no matter how difficult or far-fetched those dreams may seem to you.

Ask the person what options he or she sees in the present that will take them toward what they are aiming for. What actions could they take now that will lead in the direction they want to go? Encourage baby steps rather than monumental measures. It is the consistency of the forward movement that is important.

People who feel they are gaining more and more of the essential qualities that they want in their life are more positive, cooperative, and happier than people who feel hopeless about obtaining a greater degree of fulfillment. If you have employees, ask them how their job supports what they want for themselves in their lives. Their conscious awareness of how their work contributes to their personal fulfillment will help inspire and motivate them. As part of a job interview, ask the prospective employee what qualities they want in their life overall and how the job might contribute toward obtaining those. If money is the only reason to accept the job, the person will be less of an asset than an employee who can also gain in personal fulfillment.

Help waylay fears by emphasizing the power of choice and staying in the present moment.

Looking too far ahead triggers fear in people. What will I do if . . . ? Looking to the future and not knowing where the road is leading or what means will be available to provide for needs brings up insecurities. To help quell the doubts of a loved one in your life, refocus them to the present. Point to the blessings that are here now: good health, a roof overhead, food on the table, friends, etc. "You are okay now and that is what is important." By focusing on how their needs are being met now, you will reassure them that their needs will also be provided for in the future.

For a person who is afraid to move ahead, help him or her to define what they want for themselves. Ask: Is there a dream they are yearning for? What qualities will the realized dream give to them in their life? What would it feel like if they had what they imagine they want? Ask them to make the choice to have these qualities in their life now. What is a small step that would move them toward what they want? Have them list all the options they see possible. Push through their limitations by suggesting some frivolous alternatives or variations and combinations of the already listed options.

Go to Peru.

Go to Peru in January.

Go to Peru in June.

Go to Peru with a friend.

Go to Peru on an organized tour.

Go to Peru with a friend on an organized tour in January.

Stay home.

Have them pick the option that feels (not thinks) the best. Now ask, "What is a first small step you can take toward achieving this option?"

Often it is the timing of an action that will make a difference. When a person does not want to go forward with an action now, ask when would it feel better to take the action? Assure the person that if he or she doesn't want to take advantage of an opportunity now, another will come along. It is important for all of us to learn to trust our own pacing. Encourage him or her to pick a date in the future for reconsidering their options.

Guiding Children to Self-Reliance

Living Heartaculture with children is a special art in itself. Since children are not free agents, their parents, teachers or caretakers define the boundaries in which they live and the limits of their choices. To encourage the children in your care to live by their hearts, it is up to you to provide boundaries that are as wide as possible. You must also be comfortable with the options you choose, making sure they create safe boundaries for your child while not imposing crippling limitations.

Boundary: "You may play in the park either today or tomorrow but not both days."

Boundary: "Here are three clean shirts. Which one do you want to wear?"

Boundary: "Once your homework is done you can go outside to play or you may watch TV."

By offering choices to children as soon as it is practical to do so, you help them develop self-awareness and learn how to make decisions. Increase the number of choices and scope of options as the child matures: two colors of lollipops at first, four colors later on. When allowed to make as many choices about their lives as possible, children develop self-reliance and independence, expressing more and more of their authentic selves.

> *"Don't limit a child to your own learning, for he was born in another time."*
>
> *Rabbinical saying*

By being comfortable with the options you sanction, you can be impartial to whatever choices are made. This allows the child to please him or herself without trying to please you, a crucial step in living through Heartaculture. When you do have a bias, keep it to yourself unless asked to give your opinion. You can offer insights by pointing out possible outcomes of the choice, but otherwise allow the child to experience the results of his or her choice without your interference.

Child: "I don't want to go to football practice today."

Parent: "The choice is yours, but if you don't go it may affect your chances of playing in Saturday's game."

What happens when your child doesn't want to do what you want him or her to do? Perhaps it is homework. You do not want to force your son or daughter to do something they don't want to do, but you know what is in their best interest, right? If you hold that attitude, which I see as a conditioned one, you will constantly bypass your loved one's innate wisdom. True, as an adult you are in the position to know how to keep your child healthy and safe, but are you really the authority for knowing how best to gain personal fulfillment for your child? Are you truly aware of what is in your child's heart of hearts? Most likely not. Your child will not always consciously know either.

In Heartaculture I see the role of the parent not as a power over the child but as a facilitator. **The parent's role is to aid the child to become his or her own authority and act from heart-will.** In this way the child learns to follow his or her own inherent wisdom, which will lead to fulfillment of his or her destiny.

The form you want for your child may or may not be the best for realizing his potential. In the case of wanting your child to do his homework, the goal is likely to be the getting-good-grades-means-earning-a-future-income form. Your intent is for your child to be a "success" in the world as you see it. Remember that the world is filled with infinite possibilities, and that change is constantly occurring.

The form or option that worked for you may not be the best option for your child.

The form that feels best to you for your child most likely has the essences he or she needs. Allow yourself to be open to the possibility that your child, in his or her heart of hearts, knows what form will best satisfy these essences. Trust your own feelings, not thinking, to guide your child to find the best choices. In the homework example, you may ask your child why he doesn't want to do his homework, and then co-creatively arrive at an agreement that feels good to you both.

When at the end of his sophomore year of high school my son informed me that he wanted to drop out of school, I was horrified! In the Midwestern suburb where I grew up, dropping out of high school was a big no-no. It was something I would never consider. All my conditioned fears reared their ugly heads, and I prepared to talk my son out of his choice. How would he ever succeed in the job market without a high school diploma? I also lamented over the thought of his missing out on the wonderful social experiences of high school that I had experienced. Thank goodness I quickly got a grip on myself before voicing any of this. Instead, I asked him why he wanted to drop out? His reality was that he was bored. He had high scores on most of his tests, but his grades suffered because he wasn't doing the homework. He wanted to develop his creative skills by working with his innovative father. I asked him if he would miss the social life? His answer: "What social life?"

Once I recovered from my initial shock, I discussed the possibilities with my son and his father. We agreed that he would work with his father during the next school year and earn his GED in the summer while living with me.

This worked out well for him. It also helped me drop whatever future agenda I held for him and adopt the attitude that his destiny needs to be determined by the choices he wants to make, not by my desires for him.

When living Heartaculture with others, both children and adults, keep in mind that the idea is to encourage everyone to live from their authentic selves, to be their own authorities. Besides resulting in a greater sense of satisfaction and personal fulfillment for each person, a collective reward will be that the full inherent "genius" of each individual can be expressed and can contribute to the common goals and activities of the relationship, family, social group, organization or company.

This includes you! Don't think you have to limit yourself in order to allow others to live their hearts or to make it all work. Remember Heartaculture works because we are all connected at some level. When we allow our hearts to rule, they take into consideration all the other hearts. What one person wants in their heart of hearts automatically encompasses what all the other hearts want at that universal level. True harmony and synchronicity follow.

This may seem far-fetched given the current world in which we live. First experience Heartaculture for yourself. Once you internalize the principles enough to make them your natural tendency (they are!), begin to intentionally introduce them to others through your actions and language. It is "catching." When you live Heartaculture you become more relaxed, open, and accepting of other people as well as of yourself. Being authentic and taking responsibility for yourself encourages others around you to do the same. Gradually as you live Heartaculture collectively in your immediate world, you will recognize the possibilities for the planet.

How to co-create outcomes that allow the most satisfaction for everyone involved

Exercise

The next time you focus on accomplishing something specific with two or more people, use the following process. Modify the steps to suit the objective and the group. Appoint one person who will act as scribe to record the results of the steps when appropriate.

1. Name the specific purpose of the meeting. For example: "The purpose of this meeting is to decide how we want to spend our two-week vacation."

2. Ask, "Within this specific purpose, what are your individual desires or goals?" As you allow each person in turn to express their thoughts, write down the responses.

Example

Ask: "What kinds of things do you want to experience on this vacation?"

Responses: To do lots of hiking

To explore one area thoroughly

To eat different kinds of food

To have fun together

To go swimming and play on the beach

3. Allow each person, in turn, to express the qualities they would like from the end result.

Write down the responses.

Example

Ask: How do you want to feel on this vacation?

Responses: Taken care of

> Relaxed without time pressure
>
> Stimulated
>
> Connected with nature
>
> Loving with each other
>
> Excited

4. Without comments or judgments from anyone else, give each person an opportunity to suggest their ideal options for attaining the end result. These options should be in the spirit that anything is possible, that there are no limitations. Write down the responses.

Example

Ask: "If you could go anywhere on our vacation, where would you want to go?"

Responses:

> Alaska
>
> Catalina Island
>
> Disneyland
>
> Australia

5. If the group is big and there are many options expressed, have the group vote on their favorites. It may work best to give everyone two or three votes. The idea is to narrow down the options to a workable number while allowing full expression. You can vote by voice, show of hands, or slips of paper. If the group is small and there are only a few options, use them all.

6. Compare these options to the responses in Step 2. Can the options accomplish what the participants desire? Put a

check by the ones that can. These are the top options. If none of the options pass, that is they don't have the potential of fulfilling everything listed, determine the one or more options that can satisfy the most desires.

Example

Options: **Alaska Catalina Island Disneyland Australia**

Experiences Desired

	Alaska	Catalina Island	Disneyland	Australia
Hiking	✗	✗		✗
Exploring one area thoroughly	✗	✗	✗	✗
Eating different kinds of food	✗	✗	✗	✗
Having fun together	✗	✗	✗	✗
Swimming and playing on the beach	✗	✗		✗

7. Disneyland is the only option that doesn't have the potential for fulfilling all the experiences that are desired. All the others can be considered top options. Now consider these top options in light of the qualities desired in Step 3. Check off the ones that can fulfill the essences. If more than one option passes, can you use all of them? If not, take a vote to pick the option that will be used.

Example

Let's say that Alaska, Catalina Island, and Australia, the top options, each have the potential to satisfy all the desired qualities. A vote for the favorite of these options determines that Australia is the winner.

Note: If none of the options suggested fulfill enough of the desired experiences or qualities, you may need to ask for more suggestions of options or go back and evaluate the experiences and qualities desired. Are they what is really wanted?

Now make sure everyone is satisfied with the favored option. If there are any objections, discuss whether the option can be modified to eliminate objections.

Example

Someone questions the long flight time to Australia. Will this cause time pressures by cutting the time for activities? Also, a financial consideration is mentioned. The airfare for the family will be expensive and could cut into the available budget for land transporation or activities. A discussion suggests new options: Would a tour package be more economical? Would a resort or base location that offers day trips be better than renting a car and touring more of the country?

If time restrictions prevent the full satisfaction of some participants at this meeting, suggest that they keep working toward having exactly what they want. Have them create further options that could be used in addition to or could alter the chosen options. The full group could vote on these new possibilities at a later time.

Example

The person who suggested Disneyland wants to be sure that he gets the fun and thrills he was hoping for. After the meeting he looks into potential options in Australia that would satisfy his yearning. He discovers an amusement park and a jeep ride into the outback that would fulfill the qualities that he hopes for. He presents these options for consideration by the group at the next meeting.

8. Decide what the next small steps will be to progress toward the end result. In the vacation example, the next step may be to assign someone to find a specific destination, a hotel, resort or campground, and make reservations if required. Another small step may be to investigate airfares or group tours, or to create a timeline of what needs doing before departure.

The important elements to remember in this co-creative process are:

- All participants are considered authorities and have equal voice.

- Ideals are used first and then modified later as needed to include specific requirements.

- Each participant has the opportunity to express his or her thoughts and feelings for each point of consideration.

- Outcomes are aimed to feel good or "right" to all participants.

- Dissatisfactions to the outcome caused by time restrictions are acknowledged, and future suggestions for more satisfying options are encouraged.

Chapter Twelve

A Heartaculture World

If everyone lived by his or her heart, what kind of world would we have? Imagine all the people close to you doing only what they want to do when they want to do it. What pictures or thoughts immediately come to mind? If you come from the traditional worldview, one that insists we do the "shoulds" before the desires, most likely your image of a Heartaculture society will be of a non-productive and perhaps conflictive world or one that is out of control. Once you experience firsthand living by Heartaculture, you will know differently.

> *"In living from the awakened heart we all become Bodhisattvas, all servants of the Divine."*
>
> Jack Kornfield

When you trust that by following your desires you will always be in the right place at the right time for your greatest good, you experience the connectedness of a complex web of life. What the workings of this gigantic network are is the Great Mystery. I do not believe that any of us in the physical realm can know the full or absolute Truth of this wondrous enigma. We can only surmise with what we experience ourselves or from what we judge to be the truth from other people's sharing.

I do not know exactly why Heartaculture works. I only know that it does. My vision of a Heartaculture world comes from more than thirty years of consciously observing and living the path. I share this vision with you and ask that you run it through your own internal indicators to discern the truth of it for yourself.

I like to picture the Whole, all that exists, as a gigantic puzzle broken up into billions of smaller pieces. The impetus of the puzzle to have all its pieces assembled in a completed "picture" is called Universal Will. This "desire" calls each of the pieces to self-actualize and unite with all the other pieces, to come together as One to complete the puzzle.

Each of us is a piece. We are individually summoned by Universal Will through the heart-will, the deepest part of the Self, to be all that we can possibly be in order to contribute our part to the completed Whole. Individually felt, this desire of Universal Will becomes our personal true desire. Each of us yearns to express our part of the Whole in the best way possible in order that the full potential be realized. The more of the true Self we express, the more fully we manifest the potential of the completed puzzle. Via the heart-will, this universal true desire sparks our life force and fuels all our choices.

"Whoever is happy will make others happy too."

Anne Frank

On the individual personality level we each have our ego-will. This is what I call the "little will," Universal Will being the big Will. It is the mental faculty by which we consciously choose a course of action. It helps us use our individual characteristics and talents to negotiate the physical plane, and thus is an important part of realizing our potential. This is the "free" will with which we choose to take the daily actions we desire.

So that our innate urge to complete the Whole can be fully successful, the little will needs to be in league with the Universal Will. It needs to freely "want" to do what is directed by the heart-will.

Heartaculture automatically balances the two wills. As you consistently take direction from the heart-will, the ego-will gradually comes into alignment. It is a matter of training. As you become conscious of what your heart wants and choose to have it, the Universal Will can then be the main director of your choices. The two wills unite as the same motivating force. You become a "channel" for expressing Universal Will more completely, with lesser, incompatible, externally motivated desires falling by the wayside.

As you synchronize the two wills, you synchronize the physical and non-physical levels of existence. This is where the most efficient and effective choices are made. Heart-will is directing from the spiritual world and the little will is translating this motivation into the everyday, specific choices of the physical realm. You are then creating "As above, so below," heaven on Earth. You are taking "Thy Will," the God-Will, and making it "my will," your conscious choice.

> *"It is the creative potential itself in human beings that is the image of God."*
>
> *Mary Daly*

When we live by our hearts, we live by the Cosmic Heart, the Universal Will. Our individual hearts are joined in unison in the common true desire. Little by little we evolve the "I" heart into the "we" heart as we lose the sense of separation. We come into the realization that we are each expressions of the same Whole and of the same Heart. We welcome fitting together with the other pieces of the puzzle in cooperation, so that we express more of the full Self than we could ever experience as separate entities. We desire the best for others. It is in helping each other become clearer vehicles for the flow of Universal Will that we best help the Whole and ourselves to actualize.

Expressing more of the true Self increases our life force. We "lighten" up. Our vibratory rate literally increases. As each person lets go of anything that keeps him or her from expressing the true Self, the collective mental-emotional-psychic atmosphere lightens and the energy vibration of the planet increases. We become clearer mirrors for each other, able to reflect a fuller image of each other's potential and accept each other's individual expression unconditionally, without judgment. This, in turn, makes it easier to express even more of our authentic selves. We become more radiant beings as we increase the amount of heaven we manifest on Earth.

In the evolution of this Heartaculture vision, I see our current society as being in the adolescent stage. We are growing up but have not yet accepted full adult responsibility for what we are manifesting in our lives either as individuals or collectively. Outwardly we agree to adhere to the "rules" while inwardly rebelling. We want our freedom, but at the same time we want to be taken care of. We want the security and benefits that our institutions can provide, and yet we revolt against them. We use the roads and enjoy the parks our governments provide, but then we object to the taxes that maintain them. Our lives are a mix of what we want and what we begrudgingly accept.

We work in jobs that give us the income and health benefits we desire, yet tolerate an abusive boss, limited creative expression, or excessive time demands. We stay in relationships that give us companionship or amenities but not the deeper connection we long for. For the convenience of the city, we live with noise, pollution, and traffic. We accept the collective assumptions that "we can't have it all" and "to have the good, you have to accept the bad."

> *"We must accept this creative pulse within us as God's creative pulse itself."*
>
> *Joseph Chilton Pearce*

This pattern of conditioned compromise—accepting less than the whole of what we want as individuals—is not only unnecessary, it inhibits our personal potential from being realized and cripples the growth and quality of our society. By allowing our individual dreams to fall prey to a compromised reality that defines what we can or cannot have, what is possible or not, what we should or shouldn't do, is where we lose our hearts and thus the integrity of our authentic selves. It keeps us from having the better world we hope and pray for.

Doing only what you want to all the time sounds so very simple. It is simple, but it isn't always easy. The way our world is constructed where logic is king and heart is its mistress, heart is talked about as a desired companion, but demeaned when engaged. Well thought-out logic is esteemed as "intellect" and prized as a decision-making tool. Following one's heart may be admired, almost secretly, but not taken seriously as an accepted, equal partner for logic. It is an exception rather than a preferred path in our traditional culture's norm.

It takes fortitude, patience and persistence, as well as faith, to be a pioneer. Although not a new discovery, the heart path is the road least taken. When you choose to follow it, you help forge a new cultural pattern and advance the evolution of mankind. There is a long way yet to go for society to come into adulthood, but progress is made one person at a time. Your choice to take full responsibility for your experience and growth requires fortitude. It is not easy to stick by your feelings in spite of belittling or resistance by others. During the detox period, as you shift from doing the "shoulds" to following your desires, it is your persistence and patience that will serve to restore your balance. Keeping the faith as you trod the path is rewarded with the "enlightening" of your life and the satisfaction of creating a healthier environment for others.

As you rely more and more on your innate wisdom to guide your life, your gradual transformation to a radiantly happy person will affect the people in your life. By expressing your heart in everything you do, you will feel good about yourself and you will have more to give others. When you are the authority in your life, taking full responsibility for your direction and happiness, you create a field of inspiration for anyone you come in contact with. When you are secure in your belief in yourself and have confidence that the universe supports your well-being, you not only attract more good things to yourself, you also create a supportive "webbing" for others. People learn directly from you as well as through osmosis by witnessing your life.

The ripples of your radiance fan out around you and spread ever outward to affect the entire world. Granted, one person's "good vibes" seem only a drop in the universal bucket, but as you continue to live according to your heart and strengthen the confidence of others to do likewise, the ripples become waves.

We are all connected. EVERYTHING that happens affects EACH OF US on some level. Every action taken by each of us adds to or subtracts from the collective good, which takes us closer or further away from creating a heaven on Earth. What we do and how we do it projects ripples of energy into the spiritual, or unseen, atmosphere. If you doubt this, pay attention to your reactions to the people with whom you live or work and how you feel about them on any given day. Now multiply this effect by everyone on the planet! The pluses and minuses of our actions counterbalance every moment, determining the current, collective, vibrational atmosphere. In this way we are, in fact, each other's environment. We add to or subtract from each other's ease or dis-ease. Even though we don't usually acknowledge it for what it is, we can feel the joy or hurt of the Whole.

"The big challenge is to become all that you have the possibility of becoming.
You cannot believe what it does to the human spirit to maximize your human potential and stretch yourself to the limit."
Jim Rohn

Literally, your heartstrings are pulled on all the time, sometimes by big tugs but more often by whispers. When the pull is noticeable, it can be felt suddenly in the emotions, making you feel sad or irritable or especially lighthearted for no apparent reason. What you feel may be personal or more general. If it is personal, perhaps you are affected by something that has happened to an acquaintance, or to the people in your immediate surroundings, or to a loved one at a distance. If it is more general, it could be some world event or circumstance, such as a disastrous earthquake or a widespread celebration of a space victory. At times when your energy is especially low, or you are feeling emotional and there is no obvious cause, it helps to compare your feelings with others in your immediate environment. Are the people with whom you live or work experiencing similar feelings?

When people or events affect your psyche, it can manifest physically, i.e., you develop a headache or feel very tired even after a good night's sleep. Usually we rationalize about the cause of these emotional and physical indications, and try to find a remedy. On days when I feel so sleepy that I have a hard time keeping my eyes open, I poll my friends to see if they are experiencing the same thing. This was true recently when the United States military led an assault on Iraq. For at least a week, a good many of us felt exhausted and our hearts were heavy. Then suddenly one day I felt much lighter and had more energy. When I noticed the change, I turned on the radio to find out what was happening. Baghdad had been secured, resulting in an easing up of the combat. Again my friends had a similar experience; they felt their heaviness lift.

Not everyone will be aware or pay attention to these physical or emotional symptoms. Usually our lives are so busy that we don't take the time to reflect on all the nuances we feel with our emotions or bodies—nor do we need to. For the most part the stronger effects are the exception. The universal averaging of light and heavy vibes usually keeps us on an even keel.

I believe, however, that currently there exists an underlying universal sadness and tension on our planet. The disharmony and exploitation prevalent in the world is affecting us physically, emotionally and psychically and contributes to our stress, anxiety and heaviness. Since our hearts are connected through the shared primal Desire, we all do want what is best for all. Our natural viewpoint is an ecological one! If we were all true to our hearts, we would not exploit other people, or our land, or any of the Earth's creatures. Since currently we are not fully acknowledging or living by our hearts, we do not keep our actions attuned to this desire. When we are not true to ourselves, we are not true to the Whole.

The majority of us deny our spirits without realizing it. By accepting that our lives and the world will never fully be what we wish them to be, we walk in step with mediocrity. We carry on as best as we think we can, while hoping something outside of ourselves will change. Giving over our power to the people in our lives, expecting and often demanding that they make us happier, causes us to deny our innate power to manifest whatever we need for our own fulfillment.

Each of us has the ability to make life more the way we wish it to be right now. You do not have to wait for permission or for someone else to take the next step for you. You can choose now to take full responsibility for your life's fulfillment and satisfaction. The universe will support you fully if you allow it to. **Your true power is in becoming your authentic Self in the highest sense and in living your best potential, moment-to-moment.**

> *"Whatever God's dream about man may be, it seems certain it cannot come true unless man cooperates."*
> *Stella Terrill Mann*

Imagine if each person was committed to taking only the actions that were true to his or her heart? What a different world it would be! Can you imagine a world where parents, teachers, CEOs, and governments encourage "following your heart" as a decision-making preference? The ramifications of such a transformation are immense. What would heaven on Earth look like?

I like to believe that if each of us expressed our true Hearts all the time, we would have a world of peace and harmony, and we would know each other's hearts and have nothing to hide because we would not be judged. We would be accepted as we are, with unconditional love.

Since society would take direction from Universal Will, the ultimate Inner Authority, there would be no need for outer authorities to regulate or control anyone. The necessity for governments to pass laws to keep their constituents in check would disappear. There would be no point in having politics or plays for power. Instead, citizens would act from their heart-of-hearts; automatically all internally motivated actions would fit perfectly with everyone else's needs and desires. If indeed we each acted moment-to-moment according to our heart's direction, there might not even be a necessity for stoplights or speed limits. We would be responsive to our surroundings through our heart radar and we would all act in perfect synchronicity!

There would be no prisons, only healing centers for troubled souls. The definition of healing would be expanded to include helping the "ill" return to a balanced working relationship with his or her heart. Schools would truly be learning and sharing centers, not the conditioning "meccas" that they are now. Instead of reinforcing and furthering the programming of a mass view of reality and conformity, schools would value and encourage each person's authentic expression. They would provide tools to develop creativity and encourage adherence to personal truths while fostering co-creation for common goals and problem solving.

The power is in the "Now," and in the ongoing, daily choices you make individually and in co-creation. You can choose to perpetuate suppressed potential in your life and on the planet by making choices based in limitation, or you can decide to empower the full vitality of your spirit by adhering to the wisdom of your heart. By living the heart path, you open yourself to a more wondrous personal life and help create a new world in which mind and heart are equal and awesome partners.

Bibliography

Bernfield, Lynn. *When You Can You Will.* Los Angeles, California: Lowell House, 1992.

Blum, Ralph. *The Book of Runes.* New York, New York: St. Martin's Press, 1982.

Cameron, Julia. *The Vein of Gold:* A Journey to Your Creative Heart. New York, New York: Jeremy P. Tarcher/Putnam, 1996.

Case, Paul Foster. *The Tarot.* Richmond, Virginia: Macoy Publishing Company, 1947.

Chopra, Deepak. *The Seven Spiritual Laws of Success: A Practical Guide to the Fulfillment of Your Dreams.* Amer-Allen Publishing and New World Library, 1994.

Chopra, Deepak. *The Seven Spiritual Laws for Parents: Guiding Your Children to Success and Fulfillment.* New York: Harmony Books, 1997.

DeRohan, Ceanne. *Right Use of Will: Healing and Evolving the Emotional Body.* Four Winds Publications, 1984.

Emerson. *Essays, First Series.* Boston, Massachusetts: Houghton, Mifflin and Company, 1896.

Hawkins, M.D., Ph.D., David R. *Power Vs. Force,* The Hidden Determinants of Human Behavior. Carlsbad, California: Hay House, Inc., 2002.

Kornfield, Jack. *After the Ecstasy the Laundry: How the Heart Grows Wise on the Spiritual Path.* New York: Bantam Books, 2000.

Pearsall, Ph.D., Paul. *The Heart's Code, Tapping the Wisdom and Power of Our Heart Energy.* New York: Broadway Books, 1998.

Seuss, Dr. *Seuss-isms: Wise and Witty Prescriptions for Living from the Good Doctor.* York: Random House, 1997.

Sheehy, Gail. New Passages: *Mapping Your Life Across Time.* New York: Random House, 1995.

Wilhelm, Richard (translation). *The I Ching.* Princeton, New Jersey: Princeton University Press, 1967.

Woodman, Marion, and Elinor Dickson. *Dancing in the Flames: The Dark Goddesses in the Transformation of Consciousness.* Boston, Massachusetts: Shambhala, 1996.

About the Author

Ellen Solart, an early pioneer in the field of expansion of consciousness, has offered the public her practical and transformative approach to accessing innate wisdom for more than 30 years. As a spiritual counselor, personal growth consultant and coach, she has empowered thousands of individuals to create more joy and fulfillment in their work and personal lives. She is author of *Living Inside Out: Saying Yes to the Inner Voice* and also the founder-director of the **Heartaculture Institute**, which provides workshops, retreats, and tools for living through inner direction.

Photo: Jennifer Thornton

For more information about Ellen Solart's lectures, workshops, retreats, coaching, consulting, books, and other materials, contact:

Heartaculture Institute

HC 60, Box 4135

Mayer, AZ 86333

(928) 632-5888

www.heartaculture.com

Printed in the United States
52914LVS00007B/229-231